Creating the Global Classroom

The book examines how to begin to think like a global educator first by examining how our own histories and experiences have formed our own cultural and professional identities and second how the varied frames by which global education can be understood – pedagogical, ideological and cosmopolitan – have shaped the field. Laurence Peters connects theory and practice about global education relevant to cultivating global awareness in primary and secondary students. Rather than seeing global education as a special field separate from the other disciplines the author encourages integration of global perspectives into everything we do. Showcasing how global awareness is a developmental issue, dependent upon the student's ability to step outside of their own place-based comfort zone, this volume lays out a roadmap of major challenges and issues around instilling this awareness in students.

This book connects theory and practice about global education relevant to cultivating global awareness in primary and secondary students. From this foundation, the book engages with the challenge of integrating global perspectives within a crowded curriculum. By convincing students and teachers alike of global education's centrality, thinking globally becomes an integral component of learning across subject areas and grade levels, and this work encourages students to exercise empathy for the other and to develop critical skills to see through media distortions and 'fake news' so they can better resist the tendency of politicians in our increasingly multicultural countries to divide people along racial and ethnic lines.

Laurence Peters was born in London, England, and studied at the University of Sussex and later taught English for several years in the UK before subsequently moving to the US to pursue a doctorate degree in Education. Following a period of undergraduate teaching Laurence gained a Law Degree from the University of Maryland in 1986 and became counsel to the Subcommittee on Select Education & Civil Rights for the US House of Representatives (1986–1993) and later served as a Senior Policy Advisor to the US Department of Education (1993–2001). Dr. Peters co-wrote *From Digital Divide to Digital Opportunity*, Rowman (2003) and co-edited *Scaling Up: Lessons from Technology Based Educational Improvement*, Jossey Bass (2005) and *Global Education: Using Technology to Bring the World to Your Students*, ISTE (2009). His most recent book is *The United Nations: History and Core Ideas*, Palgrave (2015). Laurence currently teaches Global Education Policy at Johns Hopkins University and is married with three children.

Creating the Global Classroom
Approaches to Developing the Next Generation of World Savvy Students

Laurence Peters

NEW YORK AND LONDON

Cover image: woraput / Getty Images

First published 2022
by Routledge
605 Third Avenue, New York, NY 10158

and by Routledge
4 Park Square, Milton Park, Abingdon, Oxon, OX14 4RN

Routledge is an imprint of the Taylor & Francis Group, an informa business

© 2022 Laurence Peters

The right of Laurence Peters to be identified as author of this work has been asserted by him in accordance with sections 77 and 78 of the Copyright, Designs and Patents Act 1988.

All rights reserved. No part of this book may be reprinted or reproduced or utilised in any form or by any electronic, mechanical, or other means, now known or hereafter invented, including photocopying and recording, or in any information storage or retrieval system, without permission in writing from the publishers.

Trademark notice: Product or corporate names may be trademarks or registered trademarks and are used only for identification and explanation without intent to infringe.

Library of Congress Cataloging-in-Publication Data
Names: Peters, Laurence, 1952– author.
Title: Creating the global classroom : approaches to developing the next
   generation of world savvy students / Laurence Peters.
Description: First Edition. | New York : Routledge, 2022. | Includes bibliographical
   references and index.
Identifiers: LCCN 2021041230 (print) | LCCN 2021041231 (ebook) |
   ISBN 9780367643140 (Hardback) | ISBN 9780367643133 (Paperback) |
   ISBN 9781003123903 (eBook)
Subjects: LCSH: International education—United States. | Multicultural education—
   United States. | Curriculum planning—United States. | Education and globalization. |
   Teachers—Training of.
Classification: LCC LC1090 .P448 2022 (print) | LCC LC1090 (ebook) |
   DDC 370.116—dc23
LC record available at https://lccn.loc.gov/2021041230
LC ebook record available at https://lccn.loc.gov/2021041231

ISBN: 978-0-367-64314-0 (hbk)
ISBN: 978-0-367-64313-3 (pbk)
ISBN: 978-1-003-12390-3 (ebk)

DOI: 10.4324/9781003123903

Typeset in Times New Roman
by Apex CoVantage, LLC

To my grandchildren, Julia, Sofia and Benjamin, may they lead creative lives and show others the way that we can all live together in peace and harmony.

Contents

Acknowledgments	viii
Introduction	1
PART ONE **Frameworks for Global Understanding**	5
1 Why Global Education Matters: Need for a New Paradigm	7
2 What Is 'Global Education'?	15
3 Pedagogical Perspectives	23
4 Ideological Framework	38
5 Citizenship and Human Rights	50
PART TWO **School and Classroom Approaches**	61
6 Engaging in Global Popular Culture	63
7 The Dangers of a Single Story	72
8 Maximizing the 'Global' in Global Education Technology	82
9 Global Education and School Culture	92
Afterword	102
Appendix One: Global Lesson Plans	105
Appendix Two: Immigration	113
Appendix Three: Some Sample Global Lesson Plans	117
Appendix Four: Global Collaborative Connections	130
Bibliography	134
Index	136

Acknowledgments

Thanks to Juliana Mae-Neves for her assistance and to many of the other Johns Hopkins University students who contributed to the lesson plans contained here. Thanks also to my wife Michele and daughter Emma for their patience with me during the writing process.

Introduction

"We have now run out of time. The decisions we make in the next few decades will shape the future of life itself, and we can make these decisions based only on our current worldview. If this generation lacks a comprehensive view of the cosmos, the future will be decided at random."

Yuval Harari[1]

"Human beings across time and continents are more alike than they are different. The central question about human behavior is not why do these people do this or act in that way, now or in ages past, but what is that human beings do when faced with a given circumstance?"

Isabel Wilkerson[2]

"One may also observe in one's travels to distant countries the feelings of recognition and affiliation that link every human being to every other human being."

Aristotle, *Nicomachean Ethics*, 1155a 21–2, cited in Nussbaum, 1993: 242

The Meaning of 'Global'

Martin Luther King Jr. once said, "We must learn to live together as brothers or perish together as fools." The great civil rights leader's words have never been more true – in an age when politicians encourage us to believe that our differences (whether they be skin color, nationality, or gender) are paramount we all suffer in terms of increased suffering and violence towards the so-called 'other.' Schools, created in an age when nation states were just emerging, make it easy to ignore these important truths. They tend to prefer, as the Nigerian writer and feminist Chimamanda Ngozi Adichie might put it, the telling of a single story. A story written from a nationalistic perspective that trades in stereotypes that is full of heroes and villains and as Adichie puts it, "pays scant attention to the ways things have always ended badly when we forget to if not live together like brothers – at least talk together and try to understand each other."[3] If we are going to live together like brothers in a multipolar world we will have to accept that there is more than one story – more than one way of seeing reality. In doing this we also respect the storyteller and the experience they bring to the table and that is the beginning of securing trust as the gateway to understanding and cooperation.

This book is premised on the need for schools to understand how to shift gears from living in a monocultural and single story world to a multicultural multi-story world. It is a hard change to make but students are already expressing their discomfort with the old order. Exposed to an unprecedented amount of news and images about the world that exist beyond the classroom walls they fear that they are unprepared for a future in which they see politicians ignoring these realities and the urgency of taking action. According to one survey, they "believe their generation has a responsibility to better the planet, yet only half feel ready to better the world around them." They are not looking to school to make them perfect world citizens but at least to ready them for

DOI: 10.4324/9781003123903-1

2 *Introduction*

the future on a personal level.[4] As one 16-year-old student told the *Washington Post*, "It's like a dystopian novel to grow up seeing the world fall apart around you and knowing it's going to be the fight of your lives to make people stop it."[5] She joins 57% of students who feel that thinking about climate change makes them afraid with just two in ten students who feel they know "a lot" about climate change. To say that students today feel somewhat helpless and unprepared for their futures may not be an overstatement as young people try to sort through on their social media a barrage of information, much of it false, incomplete, or outright dangerous. It has never been as important for schools to help their students develop a global perspective but the challenge is how to do so with a curriculum that elevates separate subjects over interdisciplinary understanding and nationalistic stories over universalist ones.

Clearly the institution of school is deeply rooted within not just a nationalistic but also paternalistic culture. Schools are supposed to develop good citizens but that is often citizens who are conformist and who do not question the master narratives. We cannot change that system overnight since it has served powerful societal interests for a long period of time, but we must do more to respond to our students' need for a more realistic picture of the world. If we are to succeed in this task we must be more open to the world – that means when we discuss America we tell the complete story of how the country was founded and with an openness to those people with multiple ethnic backgrounds who have stories to tell about both conquest and colonization. We also need to find space to welcome more of the world into the classroom – not just using flag days or food festival days but to open up the classroom doors to voices from other parts of the world so students can get to know their peers from other countries and discover that despite language or cultural differences they have far more in common with them than they may have first believed.

One of our goals as educators must be however imperfectly to help students make sense of this dynamic world for themselves. For example, what is our connection with topics like global warming? A recent report by the UN International Organization for Migration (IOM) predicts that in 30 years from now, "one in nine people will have been forced to flee their homes due to climate change and 21.5 million people will be forcibly displaced due to climate change every year."[6] These kinds of statistics should indicate that the world's traffic lights are flashing amber – but we don't as a species tend to respond well to slow-moving emergencies. Our DNA was built for immediate threats – threats we can both see, hear, feel and touch. Climate change is not one of these and so this slow and silent catastrophe is not part of the daily or weekly news cycle. Even as we watched many parts of California on fire in 2019 and a few months later, fires in Australia burning up hundreds of millions of acres before they were fully extinguished, the media will make only passing references to climate change. If the media either will not or cannot do the job then educators must.

Since this is the generation that will be the most affected by climate change they need to be informed of options to address the crisis and its many knock-on effects. Is the Global North which continues to burn the most carbon, more than the Global South, more responsible for helping the Global South deal with the consequences of hundreds of years of mass carbon extraction and consumption? Our role is not to preach but to simply help students decide for themselves what our responsibility (as both Americans and as citizens of the world) should be. We must help our students ask and answer the hard questions such as whether they agree with Greta Thunberg, the young Swedish environmental activist who said during the plenary session of the 2018 United Nations Climate Change Conference that today's world leaders were "not mature enough to tell it like it is" and went on to accuse them of stealing her dreams and their childhoods with their "empty words." Her words went viral as she commented that we "are in the beginning of a mass extinction" and all they could talk about "is money and fairy tales of eternal economic growth." Students at least need to hear her resounding *How dare you!*[7] A modern day *j'accuse* type of indictment of our collective failure to come to terms with the full tragedy of climate change. Today's students need to understand that while many of these questions do not have easy answers they need to engage in discovering some of the solutions that make sense to them. We should be clear that this approach runs counter to the way schools were founded as state-run institutions that were seen as responsible for acculturation as well as to ensure that society had a supply of factory, office and agricultural workers.

Assisting students understand their troubled environment is premised on a different understanding of the school's function which is to help students prepare for their future – to give them the tools they need to move forward and help prepare for the critical decisions they will need to make as they enter a far more interdependent world than their parents inhabited. In doing so students must rediscover an old idea that we as well as being Americans (or any other nationality) are also citizens of the world. As John Donne said so wisely,

> No man is an island,
> Entire of itself,
> Every man is a piece of the continent,
> A part of the main.
> If a clod be washed away by the sea,
> Europe is the less.
> As well as if a promontory were.

These expressions of our common humanity go back even further – to at least 5th-century Athens when Diogenes replied to a question thrown at him about what city he was a citizen of, to which he replied, "I am a citizen of the world," and so giving birth to a cosmopolitan movement that was echoed when Bartolomé de Las Casas, who came to Cuba in 1509 as a Spanish chaplain and fiercely objected to the genocidal cruelties and proclaimed, "All the races of the world are men. . . . Thus, the entire human race is one."[8] These voices were few and far between, given that the world's religious leaders, from Moses, Jesus and Muhammad not to mention the Buddha and Confucius never made any racial or national distinctions in their work or their beliefs. It may be hard for students to understand that we can be both citizens of the world and citizens of a particular country and it is only after you explain to them that you can be a Dodgers fan as well as a Michigander or Virginian, a New Yorker and a tennis fan that people get it. We are all human beings first. To underline this point something remarkable but not well covered by the news media happened in 1987 when a group of geneticists published a surprising study in the authoritative journal *Nature*. As Josh Clark writes in the *How Stuff Works* blog,

> after taking DNA samples from 147 people, they found an astonishing fact that all of us, every person on earth can trace their lineage back to a single common female ancestor who walked the planet around 200,000 years ago. We know further where this common grandmother lived who is now named Mitochondrial Eve.[9]

The takeaway from all this is that we are all cousins. The constructs around race and nationality have no basis in science.

This book is dedicated to the hope that by breaking down some of the prejudices of ages past and recognizing the need to not get trapped into a single narrative worldview we can better help our students move forward and begin their own global journeys.

Notes

1. Harari, Y. (2018). *21 lessons for the 21st century.* New York: Spiegel and Grau, p. 208.
2. Wilkerson, I. (2020). *Caste: The origins of our discontents.* New York: Random House, p. 387.
3. *Danger of a single story*, from TED Global Talk, 2009. Retrieved July 12, 2021, from www.ted.com/talks/chimamanda_ngozi_adichie_the_danger_of_a_single_story/transcript?language=en

4 *Introduction*

4. *Wise global education barometer: Youth perceptions on their education and their futures*, January 2020. Retrieved July 12, 2021, from www.ipsos.com/en/wise-global-education-barometer-2020
5. Kaplan, S., & Guskin, E. (2019). Most American teens are frightened by climate change, poll finds, and about 1 in 4 are taking action. *Washington Post*, September 16. Retrieved July 12, 2021, from www.washingtonpost.com/science/most-american-teens-are-frightened-by-climate-change-poll-finds-and-about-1-in-4-are-taking-action/2019/09/15/1936da1c-d639-11e9-9610-fb56c5522e1c_story.html?fbclid=IwAR040PV_09WlbPuNmyXFrVLee8ty5mxJDm3N2XwmZu8MsvEFiUR2-ZGJSE8
6. Interpress Service. (2017). *Climate migrants might reach one billion by 2050*, August 21. Retrieved from https://reliefweb.int/report/world/climate-migrants-might-reach-one-billion-2050
7. Thunberg, G. (2019). Transcript: Greta Thunberg's speech at the UN Climate Action Summit. *NPR.org*, September 23. Archived from the original on 3 October 2019. Retrieved September 27, 2019.
8. Cited in Carozza, P. G. (2003). From conquest to constitutions: Retrieving a Latin American tradition of the idea of human rights. *Human Rights Quarterly, 25*, 293.
9. Clark, J. (2008). Are we all descended from a common female ancestor? *How Stuff Works Blog*. Retrieved July 12, 2021, from https://science.howstuffworks.com/life/evolution/female-ancestor.htm

Part One

Frameworks for Global Understanding

1 Why Global Education Matters

Need for a New Paradigm

Conventional Framing

Global education can provide an extra dimension to lessons, particularly when there is an obvious world event to discuss but it is hard work to integrate it into an already over-crowded curriculum.

Reframing

To fully prepare our students for an interdependent and multicultural world we must challenge ourselves to do more than gesture to the fact that we occupy a diverse and dynamic planet. We must reimagine the traditional 20th-century nationally centered approach and infuse a global perspective throughout the curriculum.

Guiding Questions

1. Why do all students need more global awareness to be fully prepared to thrive in today's interdependent world?
2. Why is global education needed to provide more curriculum relevance to today's anxious students?
3. How are some futuristic looking schools around the world responding to the new global realities?
4. Why does increased student cultural diversity increase the need for global education?

Why All Students Need More Global Awareness to Be Fully Prepared to Thrive in Today's Interdependent World

Yuval Harari, the noted best-selling historian, writes in his most recent book, *21 Lessons for the 21st Century*, about the unrealistic curriculum he was exposed to growing up in his native Israel. Harari describes with a degree of bitterness how his education shortchanged his understanding of the real world. The nationalistic view of the world where he was "taught almost nothing about China, India or Africa" seemed designed to make him a good Israeli soldier ready to die for his country but the cost of this approach, with only a few mentions of the Roman Empire, the French Revolution and the Second World War, left him perplexed – "these jigsaw pieces (did) not add up to any overarching narrative."[1] It's a problem experienced not just by Israelis; most curriculum approaches throughout the world suffer from this egocentric approach. School textbook narratives leave students with the impression that their countries can do no wrong. National

DOI: 10.4324/9781003123903-3

8   *Frameworks for Global Understanding*

or religiously based narratives also tend to play down the level of intolerance and persecution necessary to maintain power and so subtly normalize arrogant attitudes to foreigners. They also blind students to the understanding that the leaps in our growth as a world civilization were not undertaken by any single country. If you overlook the contribution of the Asian empires to civilization and only focus on the western Biblical tradition you naturally ignore that the fact that hundreds of years before the Biblical prophets or Jesus walked the earth there were ancient civilizations that developed their own social ethics that were remarkably simple and abided by for thousands of years. For example students in the West do not even come across the words or works of Confucius (551–479 BCE) who called for a code of ethics based on the golden rule, "What you do not wish for yourself, do not do to others." Or the Emperor Ashoka who ruled a racially diverse Empire that encouraged him to issue an Edict for Tolerance that included the following, "Whoever praises his own religion, due to excessive devotion and condemns others with the thought 'Let me glorify my own religion' only harms his own religion."[2]

If cultures are dismissed or treated as only stepping stones to some greater glory of our own we damage the possibilities of a full respect for other cultures and the people who share their values. For cultures are ultimately the representation of entire peoples, their ways of life as well as their beliefs and our first move must be to respect them and then begin to take steps to understand them. We will need all these abilities if we are to effectively face the major challenges that the world will face in the future – from the growth of artificial intelligence and its effect on jobs through to global pandemics, terrorism and cybercrime. These problems will be global in nature and will require countries to cooperate in new unprecedented ways. To pretend to students, even by inference, that any particular nation state can by itself address any of these challenges is the height of foolishness. Each culture has something to contribute to the human tapestry. Take the amazing discovery of Messenger RNA that was the underlying technology that produced the Covid19 vaccine. It was the work of the Hungarian-born scientist Katalin Karikó who was working in the US and her longtime and American collaborator Drew Weissman helped create the Moderna vaccine. Meanwhile in Mainz, Germany, Turkish native Ugur Sahin formed a company BioNTech which licensed technology developed by Karikó and her collaborator Weissman, eventually hiring Karikó as senior vice president to help oversee its mRNA work. Then the first cases of Covid were identified in China and after isolating the virus from patients, Chinese scientists on Jan. 10 posted online its genetic sequence.

> Because companies that work with messenger RNA don't need the virus itself to create a vaccine, just a computer that tells scientists what chemicals to put together and in what order, researchers at Moderna, BioNTech, and other companies got to work.[3]

This was a worldwide collaboration and it exemplifies the world we now inhabit.

Why Global Education Is Needed to Supply Curriculum Relevance to Today's Anxious Students

Future shock was a term futurologist Alvin Toffler first coined in a magazine article in the 1960s. He defined it as the anxiety brought on by "too much change in too short a period of time." We might look back with some nostalgia to the 1960s' relatively slow pace of change then compared to today but his terminology seems even more accurate as we learn to apply gene splicing, artificial intelligence and digital technologies to every aspect of life. Toffler also coincidentally coined the term 'information overload' which summarizes the way we are barraged with news and information from our phones, computers, newspapers, TV and radio and we are regularly exhorted to take 'holidays' from our devices. Toffler urged us to "search out totally new ways to anchor ourselves, for all the old roots religion, nation, community, family, or profession are

Why Global Education Matters 9

now shaking under the hurricane impact of the accelerative thrust." The new identities we seek are no longer rooted in nation states but increasingly tribes of interest that span across borders. Today commodities, brands, sports and entertainment are global phenomena and schools still are wedded to an older nation-centric view of the world. We must help our students understand the way, as Toffler predicted the world will increasingly be full of disposable products and workers who, unless they can learn the new skills necessary, will also be disposable. "The illiterate of the 21st century will not be those who cannot read and write," he wrote, "but those who cannot learn, unlearn, and relearn." While schools cannot provide all the answers they can help students understand what are the questions they need to ask themselves – as they search for meaning in this fast-changing world.

The current curriculum is not built to answer many of these students' questions. Arjun Appadurai, an Indian-born anthropologist, wrote in his best-known work "Disjuncture and Difference in the Global Cultural Economy" that he believes the world is now best understood as a series of five 'scapes' or flows: ethnoscapes, technoscapes, ideoscapes, financescapes and mediascapes. Appadurai's concept allows us to understand more concretely national boundaries are no longer that relevant for understanding how the communities we inhabit are changing. Our conventional curriculum that divides subjects up into vertical categories – heavily influenced by nationalistic concerns like most other institutions in society – cannot begin to keep up with the fast moving changes. So with regard to media scapes, how do you explain for example the growth of media empires that now span the globe and their intersection with multinational corporations that own or sponsor many of them? In the case of ethnoscapes, why do so-called 'global citizens' like Rupert Murdoch get to own vast portions of media companies across different continents and even gather enough power to influence elections and yet those who try to legally migrate from one country to another are made to feel like second-class citizens without the right to live permanently in the country or even to vote?

With regard to technoscape, how is it possible that a gadget like the latest iPhone causes long lines to snake around Apple stores in almost every country and that people will pay a premium for the pleasure of updating a piece of technology that contains a fine upgrade on their ability to take a high-definition photograph? How on the other end of the production line do we countenance the exploitation of workers who make these commodities under labor conditions that have resulted in many suicides?

Financescapes can best be understood as to what happens when the marketplace is redrawn from local and regional enterprises to companies that can sell anywhere and, in reducing both the cost of production and distribution, can make vast profits by undercutting the prices of those companies unable to command such huge markets or manage such vast supply chains.

Ideoscapes are propelled by a social media environment that works virally so that one meme (video or photo whether sent via Facebook, YouTube, Instagram or TikTok) can travel the world and back within seconds creating headlines around the world, particularly if the meme involves a celebrity in a compromising situation.

> Kelsey Timmerman, a globe-trotting journalist wanted to know more about how his clothing was made. He turned his curiosity into a best-selling book finding out how 97% of our clothes are made and found some disturbing results. For example, in Bangladesh, he went undercover and found that children were producing his T-shirts and that his all-American blue jeans were made in Cambodia and that some workers were struggling to live on less than a dollar a day.
>
> T-shirt manufacturing allows a student to see all five of Appadurai's scapes in action. The ideoscape makes it trendy to say the least for young people in particular to have on

10   *Frameworks for Global Understanding*

> hand a variety of T-shirts that express some part of their personality. The finance scope allows a US or other foreign company to contract with a production facility in another country who offers the lowest bid. The whole transaction is enabled by the technoscape that provides the mass manufacturing machinery and the communication software to regulate supply and demand. You can view the migration from the rural villages to the T-shirt factory through the lens of the ethnoscape while the mediascape helps us understand how these T-shirts are marketed.

Students are demanding that their education prepares them for a future everyone feels is going to be unpredictable – refreshing an old deck of cards into many new patterns.

According to the World Bank, over 40% of the global population is under the age of 25.[4] This statistic also includes our students who will be part of a generation that will face both the predicted shocks caused by climate change and a new gig economy who will not be able to rely on lifetime employment contracts. These new workers will be entering an expanding knowledge universe – a universe where the demand for skills to take advantage of the new knowledge will be relentless. In order to keep up, even high school graduates will need to engage in a lifetime of learning if they expect to sustain a middle-class lifestyle. Many of those jobs will be tied to international trade; today 20% are, and the forecast is for the percentage to grow as developed markets become saturated and new markets continue to emerge in South East Asia and beyond. It is not surprising therefore to see a UK report, *The Global Skills Gap: Preparing Young People for the Global Economy*, finding that employers rate knowledge and awareness of the wider world as more important than a candidate's exam results.[5] Students need to know that people who can work in a global workforce and lead a diverse team will be in higher demand as more and more companies form teams stretching across different continents. The old model of schooling that required the students to be passive and trust that the adults teaching them know best is over. They are demanding that their curriculum be relevant and connected to their lives.

They are demanding more relevance since they no longer want to be spectators to a problem that deeply involves them but become part of the solution, students today must know the significance of the global market. They experience it in their own lives as various music, videos and memes go viral and they are more aware that their clothes and their food are made elsewhere and their future work may well be sourced in another country.

How Are Schools Around the World Responding to the New Global Realities?

Across the globe some of our best schools are aware that they need to introduce innovative curricula to address today's world, not yesterday's and prepare tomorrow's graduates and future employees.[6]

- Finland South Tapiola High School is considered one of the best schools in Finland. One of the reasons it stands out is due to the Young Entrepreneurship Programme which provides groups of students an opportunity to form their own companies and enter in national competitions.
- Bali's Green School is located in the jungles of Bali, because it wants to be among other things a global model for sustainability. Inside the bamboo walls students learn practical ways to apply their academic knowledge to solving real-world problems, culminating in a capstone project ending up as a TED-like talk.

- Denmark's Ørestad Gymnasium is set inside a cube that enables open studying environments instead of traditional digitally infused classrooms, where students are expected to actively problem solve with the teacher acting more as mentor and consultant than a 'sage on a stage.'
- AltSchool in San Francisco's Silicon Valley is one of a series of 'micro schools' focused on project-based learning that aims to develop students' interests as negotiated between the family, teacher and student. Students move from various rooms or 'stations' during the day, sometimes working on their own passion projects and sometimes reflecting on their activities.[7]
- The Steve Jobs School in Amsterdam, Netherlands, named after the legendary founder of Apple computers is dedicated to the proposition that students need to learn at their own pace. Students' iPads which are used to study, play, share work, prepare presentations and communicate with others as well as monitor performance are the foundation of the approach.[8]

The future is here, but as someone said, "it's just unevenly distributed." These schools are pointing the way to an exciting future for schooling that will resist a one-size-fits-all approach so characteristic of the last century and begin to formulate different kinds of pathways for students. Meanwhile, each of us in our own classroom, schools and other institutions must continue to find ways to create curriculum approaches more responsive to our times and our interdependent globe.

Why Increased Student Cultural Diversity Increases the Need for Global Education

The US is becoming like many other nations in the West – more diverse. According to a recent Brookings Report

> the share of U.S. 15-year-old students with immigrant backgrounds increased from 18% in 2000 to 32% in 2015. One out of 10 K-12 public school students is considered limited English proficient (LEP), and about 70% were born in the U.S. and are U.S. citizens.[9]

Our classrooms reflect these trends as mostly monocultural teachers are confronted with unprecedented amounts of diversity. It is quite easy to see this as a negative even though schools are given additional funds to assist bilingual education. It is maybe hard to see these demographic changes as opportunities rather than burdens for an already overtaxed system but with some support and a positive globally minded mentality they make clear some new realities. First that we no longer live in a monocultural world and that we have to try to develop an alternative to the largely Anglo curriculum inherited from the days when the British empire was dominant.

"A multipolar world has emerged. It's the major trend of our time, which is for the first time allowing every person on the planet to become, in a cultural sense, an actor on the world stage."

(Didier Billion, French political scientist)[10]

Here we may need to be reminded that we live in a democracy within a multicultural society. We need to develop a new global ethic in which students feel that their multiple ethnic and national identities are no longer denied in an effort to absorb them into a metaphorical 'melting pot.' This ethic must include recognition that everyone (sometimes a generation or more back) is from somewhere else and that we all share a destiny with everyone on the rest of the planet. But we

12 *Frameworks for Global Understanding*

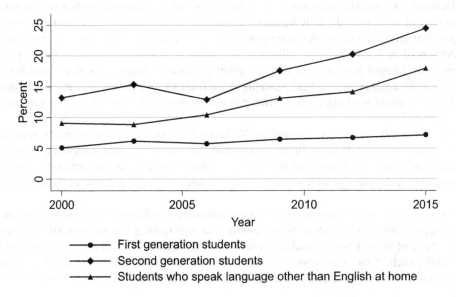

Figure 1.1 Percent of 15-year-old US students with immigrant backgrounds, 2000–2015

cannot stop there. If the traditional approach was to try to meld students into a bland all-American identity, the new ethic must be about allowing students to fully grasp their roles as global citizens and as enhancers of universal human rights.

As Slovenian philosopher, Slavoj Zizek states,

> The threat today is not passivity but pseudo-activity, the urge to "be active," to "participate," to mask the nothingness of what goes on. People intervene all the time, "do something"; academics participate in meaningless "debates," and so forth, and the truly difficult thing is to step back, to withdraw from all this.[11]
>
> (Zizek, 2009)

By ignoring the diversity all around us and continuing to teach as though our students' cultural and ethnic backgrounds were irrelevant we, whether subconsciously or consciously, take power away from them and reduce their self-efficacy which is so vital to academic achievement. As Howard details,

> In repeated studies, these researchers found that three factors have a major effect on students' motivation and performance: their feelings of belonging, their trust in the people around them, and their belief that teachers value their intellectual competence. This research suggests that the capacity of adults in the school to form trusting relationships with and supportive learning environments for their students can greatly influence achievement outcomes.

It is these feelings of belonging that globally minded teachers have to take seriously. The relentless need to ensure that students are fully able to regurgitate information on a test often prevents us from attending to the basic needs to develop these trusting caring relationships. Some counties that have experienced rapid growth (mainly due to the influx of immigrants) are beginning to wake up to the need to shift instruction to at least recognize students' complex experience with culture – which often means they deal with the clash between their family values and beliefs and those of American society.[12]

Because global education has been so hard to sustain in many schools but even more retains its relevance, integrating it effectively in a curriculum presents both a challenge and an opportunity for every teacher.

Conclusion

We live in a very fearful world, particularly the one that came after 9/11. We also live in one that is drowning in information but starved of meaning. The danger is that students will become overwhelmed with the choices and become passive or even 'inactive' in the face of the sense of complexity. We need to remind ourselves that the point of teaching global education is not to have students take sides but rather to assist students to discover their own voice, their own viewpoint on these complex issues that affect them now and certainly into their future. If there is any global education ideology it is that teachers need to embody the idea that understanding comes through the melding of a variety of perspectives and that no one approach to any issue, no one view advanced by a single interest group or country can be absolute or determinative. It is easy to lose sight of this basic idea and the way that this multicultural approach is the best preparation for students to become globally competent.

We need rapid change in at least five basic areas:

1. A monocultural and mono-national focus to a multicultural and multilateral approach. This includes both a shift in attitude regarding the teaching of subjects like history and social studies but also an openness to teaching more than one other language.
2. Rarely visiting (either virtually or physically) people from other cultures to one where those from those other cultures are regularly welcomed into the classroom.
3. A strictly academic model of school where classrooms treat students as mainly there to consume content, divorced from world problems and issues to a world where students use their knowledge to act in the world.
4. Schools that continue to underplay the existential threats of global issues such as climate change, pandemics, migration and overestimate the power of national governments to solve these issues alone.
5. Single disciplinary approaches to solving the complex global problems referenced in #4 to multidisciplinary approaches.

There are many reasons to believe that we need to teach global education because this generation of students are particularly vulnerable to what Alvin Toffler once referred to as "future shock." Future shock caused by rapid globalization will mean that students need to adapt even faster to the changes ahead and can only do so if they are prepared by teachers who are aware of the stakes in play.

Notes

1. Harari, Y. (2018). *21 lessons for the 21st century*. New York: Spiegel and Grau, p. 187.
2. *The edicts of Ashoka* (Dhammika, V., Trans.). Buddhist Publication Society, 1994. Retrieved July 12, 2021, from www.cs.colostate.edu/~malaiya/ashoka.html
3. Garde, D., & Saltzman, J. (2010). The story of mRNA: How a once-dismissed idea became a leading technology in the Covid vaccine race. *Boston Globe*, November 10. Retrieved July 12, from www.statnews.com/2020/11/10/the-story-of-mrna-how-a-once-dismissed-idea-became-a-leading-technology-in-the-covid-vaccine-race/
4. Gray, A. (2018). *What you need to know about the world's youth, in 7 charts*. Retrieved July 12, 2021, from www.weforum.org/agenda/2018/08/what-you-need-to-know-about-the-worlds-young-people-in-7-charts/

14 *Frameworks for Global Understanding*

5. British Council. (2011). *The global skills gap: Preparing young people for the new global economy.* Retrieved July 12, 2021, from https://think-global.org.uk/wp-content/uploads/dea/documents/BusinessPoll_online_TG.pdf
6. Weller, C. (2015). The 13 most innovative schools in the world. *Business Insider*, October 5. Retrieved from www.businessinsider.com/the-13-most-innovative-schools-in-the-world-2015-9
7. Robinson, M. (2015). A former Google exec created a school to transform the way we teach kids. *Business Insider*, September 8. Retrieved from www.businessinsider.com/altschool-max-ventilla-2015-8#classrooms-are-treated-like-stations-rather-than-designated-areas-for-particular-grade-levels-and-students-move-from-room-to-room-throughout-the-day-its-especially-important-for-micro-schools-tomaximize-spaceso-that-afour-room-schoolhouse-doesnt-feel-cramped-19
8. InnoveEdu. *Steve Jobs School and the Dutch Government.* Retrieved July 13, 2021, from www.innoveedu.org/en/steve-jobs-school
9. Sanchez, C. (2017). *English language learners: How your state is doing.* Retrieved July 13, 2021, from www.npr.org/sections/ed/2017/02/23/512451228/5-million-english-language-learners-a-vast-pool-of-talent-at-risk
10. Quoted in Kimmelman, M. (2010). Pardon my French. *New York Times*, April 21. Retrieved July 13, 2021, from www.nytimes.com/2010/04/25/arts/25abroad.html
11. Pais, A., & Costa, M. (2020). An ideology critique of global citizenship education. *Critical Studies in Education*, *61*(1), 1–16. https://doi.org/10.1080/17508487.2017.1318772
12. See Howard, G. (2007). As diversity grows, so must we. *Educational Leadership*, *64*(6). Responding to Changing Demographics Pages 16–22. Retrieved July 12, 2021, from www.ascd.org/publications/educational-leadership/mar07/vol64/num06/As-Diversity-Grows,-So-Must-We.aspx

2 What Is 'Global Education'?

> **Conventional Framing**
>
> Global education is a fluid term that encompasses a broad set of approaches that range from multicultural education to climate change.
>
> **Reframing**
>
> Global education has evolved over time and now encompasses a variety of approaches whose commonality is a bias towards providing students with the knowledge and skills necessary for them to take action in the world.

Guiding Questions

1. What were the origins of global education?
2. How does the global competency movement connect with global education?
3. How does global competency connects with assessment frameworks?

What Were the Origins of Global Education?

Global education is a recent and composite term – composed from a number of approaches that all have the end result of reminding students that they live in an interdependent world and can exercise their agency to influence its direction.

The term global education took off (as can be seen from the N-Gram graph shown in Figure 2.1) in the 1970s when both the environmental and peace movements started asking hard questions about the role of the curriculum in helping students understand their role in these larger issues.[1]

A Catalytic Event

Arguably the initial spark that set the global education movement in motion was provided by the explosion of interest in the publication of one book, *Silent Spring* by Rachel Carson. Carson had been concerned for a while about the widespread use of synthetic pesticides and attracted a community of government researchers and scientists who also had similar concerns about their deadly environmental impact. The book published in 1962 set in motion a remarkable shift in public opinion away from the idea that we could inject tons of toxic chemicals into the environment with impunity to a concept that we need to respect nature's ecological balance. The case of DDT was the critical example; while it wiped out malaria-infected mosquitoes, it did so at a very high

DOI: 10.4324/9781003123903-4

16 *Frameworks for Global Understanding*

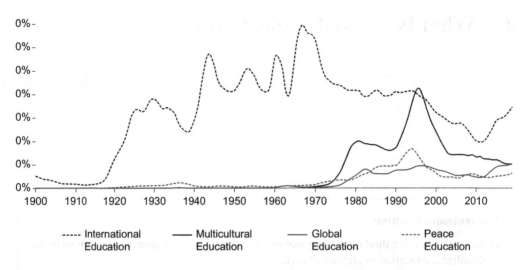

Figure 2.1 Trends in various terms related to global education between 1900–2000

cost to animal and marine life. John Kenneth Galbraith called the work among the most impactful works of western literature, and Robert Down called it "one of the books that changed America." It not only inspired the environmental movement we know today, leading to the founding in 1967 of the Environmental Defense Fund and the federal government's response to the Environmental Protection Agency (EPA) in 1970 which led the way to the chemical's banning. The DDT story forced us to revisit our most cherished beliefs that science could control nature and we could have an abundance of material goods without any environmental costs. The DDT story as described by Carson caught the public's imagination as it revealed earth's basic fragility.[2]

> These sprays, dusts, and aerosols are now applied almost universally to farms, gardens, forests, and homes – non-selective chemicals that have the power to kill every insect, the "good" and the "bad," to still the song of birds and the leaping of fish in the streams, to coat the leaves with a deadly film, and to linger on in the soil – all this though the intended target may be only a few weeds or insects. Can anyone believe it is possible to lay down such a barrage of poisons on the surface of the earth without making it unfit for all life? They should not be called "insecticides," but "biocides."

Carson's passionate outburst against knowingly sending poisons into the environment hit a strong nerve, particularly among the young. She did not pull punches; she really believed that unless we reflected on our mindless ways we would cause an unimaginable catastrophe. It gave global education a clear moral direction, setting the stage for students to actively discover ways that earth's fragile ecological balance could be preserved and sustained for future generations.

Almost a half century earlier in the aftermath of the First World War another idealistic moment had occurred when famed educator John Dewey recognized that schools had a critical role to play in preventing another catastrophe. 'Peace education' was designed as an antidote to the ideology that had glamorized war and patriotism at the expense of peaceful values such as negotiation and compromise. Dewey toured the country, lecturing on the need for a "curriculum in history, geography, and literature, . . . which will make it more difficult for the flames of hatred and suspicion to sweep over this country in the future." Instead of nationalism his peace curriculum was designed to promote 'world patriotism.'[3] Although peace education did not manage to gain much of a foothold in schools, Dewey's belief that schools could help counter a prevailing destructive societal culture was a key step in the eventual conceptualization of global education. One influential thinker in particular, a Chicago University trained anthropologist, was very aware of the way Dewey's contribution had shifted thinking about the school's potential to offer students a different perspective. Writing for the New York-based Center for War/Peace Studies in 1975, just at the moment when the progressive movement was at its height as disillusionment with the Vietnam war was setting in, Hanvey connected the pieces that were to form the basis of global education. The objective for global educators was not to sermonize about the evils of a world that may have lost sight of humane values or had only weakly grasped the ecosystem's vulnerability but rather to help students use their imaginative powers to comprehend the way global forces were shaping their world.

Hanvey's rather modest goal was to help his students grasp an 'attainable global perspective.' The term was not an easy one to unpack. For Hanvey we were always, no matter what stage in life, trying to grasp the interconnected nature of the world, but for young people that task was made all the more challenging by the constant barrage of media coverage that presented the world episodically and sensationally through headlines and images designed to provoke visceral emotions. Hanvey outlines five dimensions of a global perspective:

1. Perspective consciousness.
2. State of the planet awareness.
3. Cross-cultural awareness.
4. Knowledge of global dynamics.
5. Awareness of human choices.

In a 2004 republication of Hanvey's pioneering work, the American Forum on Global Education offers a concise distillation of Hanvey's original five dimensions:[4]

> Education for a global perspective is that learning which enhances the individual's ability to understand his or her condition in the community and the world and improves the ability to make effective judgments. It includes the study of nations, cultures, and civilizations . . . with a focus on how these are all interconnected and how they change. . . . It provides the individual with a realistic perspective on world issues, problems and prospects, and an awareness of the . . . concerns of people elsewhere in the world.
>
> (American Forum for Global Education, 2004)

Hanvey's work still serves as 'a starting place' for a number of frameworks that organizations such as the Asia Society, the International Education Consortium, the Stanley Foundation and many others have offered (Zhao, 2009, pp. 145–151; Mansilla & Jackson, 2011).[5] While global education continues to evolve as more groups seek to provide more precise definitions – some preferring to talk more about global competencies, outcomes such as the ability to master one or more of Hanvey's global dimensions – some are interested in adding more dimensions such as a global social action advocacy. The throughline is a desire to engage students in relevant action. We don't study global education because like anthropologists or ethnographers we are interested in simply exploring and describing the world's diverse cultures but because we want people at the end of the day to be motivated enough to want to do something in the world with this knowledge. This is the theme that comes through loud and clear from pioneers like Dewey and from Rachel Carson. Rather than straining after a single way to characterize global education Engel encourages us to think of global education as a kind of 'hub' for various orientations and understandings. As she explains, "discourses of global citizenship, and global competence, entail a wide range of agendas, including education for sustainability, economic competitiveness, equality and human rights, social justice, and intercultural understanding" and so challenge "any attempt to provide concrete definition for measurement purposes."[6]

18   *Frameworks for Global Understanding*

The Grand Tour: A First Taste of Global Education Undertaken by Europe's Aristocratic Elite

The Grand Tour became fashionable in the 18th century when young Oxbridge aristocrats began to tour Italy and Greece. Often these graduates would start in France and take in a few theatrical performances and then travel down to Italy, experience Venice, Rome and Florence's great architectural marvels before departing for Turkey and beginning to understand the contribution of the great Ottoman empire. The tour became a way to establish a young noble as a 'worldly' learned and civilized individual who not only possessed 'book knowledge' but a realistic grasp of what they were to understand as their classical heritage. The Grand Tour helped imprint the hierarchies of what was considered good taste in painting, wine, theater and music as well as architecture and good government. They did nothing to reduce the stereotypical views of various races.

How Does the Global Competency Movement Connect With Global Education?

The global competency movement hopes to simplify the educator's task. Instead of trying to integrate several dimensions into the curriculum, a more straightforward way of approaching the task is to look at the intended outcomes. Fernando Reimers, together with the Asia Society and the OECD, have become powerful advocates for this type of approach.[7] As Reimers states, the goal is to cultivate "the knowledge and skills people need to understand today's flat world and to integrate across disciplines so that they can comprehend global events and create possibilities to address them." These global competencies require students to possess the appropriate "attitudinal and ethical dispositions that make it possible to interact peacefully, respectfully, and productively with fellow human beings from diverse geographies." In other words these competencies should not be considered as technical skills – it is still up to teachers to develop the understanding of issues so that students are fully engaged in their efforts to attack the multiple challenges the globe faces with vigor. In the wake of 9/11 when many conservative thinkers wanted us to return to a world in which patriotic values prevented self-critical reflection and analysis, the global competency approach seemed a preferable way forward. Not only was the language of skills and competencies more in tune with the spirit of corporate America that was also interested in graduates prepared to do business in the global marketplace, it fell in line with the increased tendency to want to constantly measure and assess in the name of increased accountability.

Fernando Reimers's Key Global Competencies

1. Knowledge and understanding of global issues as well as intercultural knowledge and understanding.
2. Skills, especially analytical and critical thinking.
3. Attitudes (e.g. openness, global-mindedness, responsibility).

OECD Global Competencies

1. The capacity to examine issues and situations of local, global and cultural significance (e.g. poverty, economic interdependence, migration, inequality, environmental risks, conflicts, cultural differences and stereotypes).

---

2. The capacity to understand and appreciate different perspectives and worldviews.
3. The ability to establish positive interactions with people of different national, ethnic, religious, social or cultural backgrounds or gender.
4. The capacity and disposition to take constructive action toward sustainable development and collective well-being.

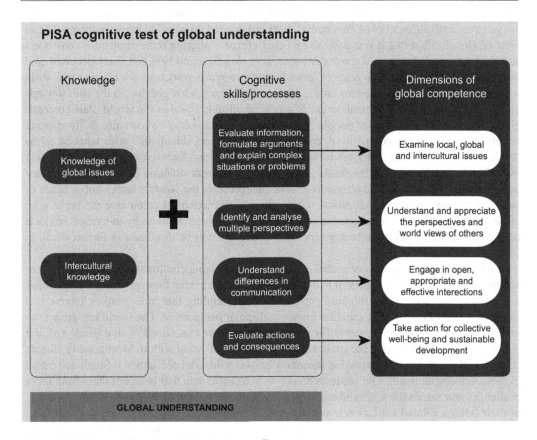

Figure 2.2 PISA cognitive test of global understanding

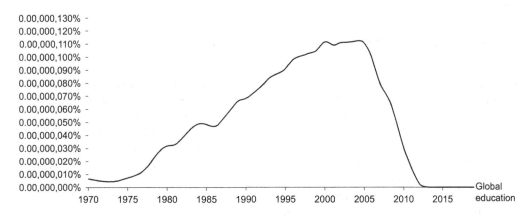

Figure 2.3 Global education mentions from 1970–2019

20 *Frameworks for Global Understanding*

This was all in marked contrast to a well-established trend that had begun in the 1980s to open up the curriculum to more global content. As can be seen in Figure 2.3, from the 1970s through to the 2000s there were increased mentions of global education year after year but a precipitous decline after 2011. Following 9/11 it became safer to talk about global competencies instead of terms like globalization and global citizenship. By 2021 with PISA's first assessment of global competency and as reflected in Figure 2.2 there was an increasing level of sophstication concerning the elements of global competency as well as an expanded recognition that economically advantaged students were provided more opportunities to refine those competencies.[8] These are not just semantic differences as Pais makes clear but opened up a divide between the neoliberal view of globalization that it was basically a benign force – offering more choice for consumers and workers – and the view of those that were more skeptical and believed that workers would lose out in the long run as the price of labor went down when workers from all over the world were forced to compete for the new online jobs. As Pais states, what gets lost in the shift towards global competencies is the development of a critical attitude towards the world. Pais contrasts global competency to prepare "people for an already given world" whose aim is "to educate people to become more competitive, entrepreneurial and individualistic" with what he terms "critical democracy," that understands the "world is a mess" and that we can make progress only by "critical engagement with the world . . . and turn the current situation into a more social just one."[9] I would propose a third alternative – one that presents the world's issues not in terms of large abstractions such as globalization, supply chains and frictionless commerce etc. but as a set of human issues that contain contradictions and need to be sorted through by individual students because there are no single right answers. This pedagogy will be discussed in further detail in Chapter 3.

Teachers who want to embrace global education are not signing up for any specific curriculum or form of assessment (those are still in developmental stages); what they are doing is responding to a need to develop critical thinkers capable of understanding that in a complex interrelated world they need to approach problems from a multipolar perspective. The world has grown too interdependent, violent and chaotic for us to accept that we can afford to live inside cultural bubbles and expect to survive the challenges this century will bring with it. Most notably climate change, global pandemics, increasing inequality between the Global North and South and a host of more unforeseen issues. Our students do not want a curriculum that insulates them from these challenges and denies the tools and capacities that will allow them to take some form of control of their futures. Global education is not the perfect solution to close the gap between handing on the traditional aspects we expect schooling to provide (such as a sense of the nation's history, literature and geography) and the skills and knowledge that our students will need to secure their futures.

How to Connect Global Competency With Assessment Framework

One of the persistent issues with regard to global education is how to measure outcomes. How do we know whether a student has the capacity to be cross-culturally literate or understand issues from different cultural viewpoints? Reimers and others have been keen to ensure that we inject a measure of rigor into global education issues so it is important to be able to develop student learning outcome measures. In their paper, "Evaluating Global Digital Education: Student Outcomes Framework," the authors provide some important indicators they regard as essential for high-quality program implementation. Their chapter on diversity is particularly helpful in suggesting ways to apply the framework to a class of 7th and 8th graders learning about diversity. As the authors argue, "middle school is the first time when students are developmentally capable of learning about diversity, and developing the attitudes and skills that will allow them to accept others as adults." One of the challenges comes from children's negative attitudes toward and misconceptions about different racial and ethnic groups (Aboud, 2008). The school has a vital role in intervening so that those attitudes are critically reflected on and rejected as prejudiced and unhelpful. There is no magic bullet to accomplish this task. Teachers must engage students in a way that allows them to self-reflect on how they assign value to people who look or talk differently from themselves. The trick is to enable students to understand for themselves their own biases and to recognize that such behavior is both natural but continues to radiate negative consequences for everyone in their community.

Appreciation for Diversity Knowledge Indicators

Awareness of how one's life and the lives of others are influenced by broader cultural and historical contexts:

1. Awareness of one's culture (behaviors, identity, beliefs).
2. Awareness of one's city and how it relates to other cities around the world.
3. Awareness of different cultures within one's school, city, region, country and world.
4. Awareness of one's identity as a citizen of one's city.

Skill Indicators

1. Ability to identify and critically reflect on stereotypes in thinking about others.
2. Ability to listen to others and discuss issues in a respectful and unbiased way.
3. Ability to ask questions when encountering different perspectives.
4. Ability to identify and critically reflect on intolerant behavior online and in person.

Conclusion

This divide may have started to grow after 9/11, following the backlash that it provoked against globalization. Public schools in particular were notably averse to controversy such as would arise if in certain communities schools would require any study of Islam or understand some of the causes of Arab rage. The theme was American exceptionalism and words such as 'globalization' and 'global citizenship' were seen as in opposition to this term that supposedly supported American values that were threatened on 9/11.[10] As Lynn Cheney (former Chairwoman of the National Endowment of the Humanities) said shortly after the attack, the notion that Americans needed to learn more about other cultures in the world, she argued, was tantamount to admitting "that the events of September 11th were our fault, that it was our failure to understand Islam that led to so many deaths and so much destruction." We have a cloudy idea of what the future looks like and in times like these our tendency is to look backwards. Our curriculum reflects this hesitation – on the one hand according to one recent study, more secondary textbooks than ever before from around the world now feature global concepts, global awareness and global competencies.[11]

Notes

1. Google Ngram Viewer or Google Books Ngram Viewer is an online search engine that charts the frequencies of any set of comma-delimited search strings using a yearly count of grams found in sources printed between 1500 and 2008 in Google's text corpora in English, Chinese (simplified), French, German, Hebrew, Italian, Russian or Spanish.
2. Carson, R. (1962). *Silent Spring*. Boston: Houghton Mifflin, p. 7.

22 *Frameworks for Global Understanding*

3. Howlett, C. (1977). *Troubled philosopher: John Dewey and the struggle for world peace.* Port Washington, NY: Kennikat Press, pp. 60–63.
4. Hanvey, R., *An attainable global perspective.* Retrieved July 14, 2021, from https://files.eric.ed.gov/fulltext/ED116993.pdf
5. Mansilla, V., & Jackson, A. (2011). *Educating for global competence: Preparing our youth to engage the world.* Asia Society & Council of Chief State School Officers. Retrieved from http://asiasociety.org/files/book-globalcompetence.pdf and Zhao, Y. (2009). *Catching up or leading the way: American education in the age of globalization.* Alexandria, VA: ASCD and Mansilla, V., & Jackson, A. (2011). *Educating for global competence: Preparing our youth to engage the world.* Asia Society & Council of Chief State School Officers. Retrieved from http://asiasociety.org/files/book-globalcompetence.pdf
6. Engel, L. C., Rutkowski, D., & Thompson, G. (2019). Toward an international measure of global competence? A critical look at the PISA 2018 framework. *Globalisation, Societies and Education, 17*(2), 117–131. https://doi.org/10.1080/14767724.2019.1642183
7. The OECD defines global competency as a

> combination of knowledge, skills, attitudes and values successfully applied to face-to-face, virtual or mediated encounters with people who are perceived to be from a different cultural background, and to individuals' experiences of global issues (i.e., situations that require an individual to reflect upon and engage with global problems that have deep implications for current and future generations).

> OECD. (2018). *Preparing our youth for an inclusive and sustainable world: The OECD PISA Global Competence Framework.* Retrieved from www.oecd.org.proxy1.library.jhu.edu/pisa/Handbook-PISA-2018-Global-Competence.pdf

8. Jackson, Tony, *The First PISA Assessment of Global Competence, Asia Society,* Retrieved from https://asiasociety.org/education/first-pisa-assessment-global-competence
9. Pais, A., & Costa, M. (2020). An ideology critique of global citizenship education. *Critical Studies in Education, 61*(1), 1–16. https://doi.org/10.1080/17508487.2017.1318772
10. See Rubin, D., & Verheul, J., *American multiculturalism after 9/11: Transatlantic perspectives,* p. 7. Retrieved from https://library.oapen.org/bitstream/handle/20.500.12657/35323/340001.pdf?sequence=1&isAllowed=y
11. Lee, S. S. (2020). Fostering "global citizens"? Trends in global awareness, agency, and competence in textbooks worldwide, 1950–2011. *Prospects, 48,* 215–236. https://doi.org/10.1007/s11125-020-09465-2. The data come from an extant dataset coded from 624 secondary-school textbooks from 80 countries between 1950 and 2011.

3 Pedagogical Perspectives

Conventional Framing

Global education is mainly about adding relevant content to the curriculum, not about responding to developmental or pedagogical issues.

Reframing

Effective global education teachers recognize that global understanding is formed of many elements, including the development of dispositions, attitudes and skills aligned both with the relevant curriculum standards as well as with student interests.

Guiding Questions

1. How do we prepare our students for the new global realities?
2. Why is it so vital to personalize global education and make it relevant to students' lives ?
3. Why is starting with experiential learning so crucial in building global competence?
4. How should we apply global education concepts to the curriculum?

How Do We Prepare Our Students for the New Global Realities?

Yuval Harari, the author of the best-selling *Sapiens* refers in his latest book, *21 Lessons for the 21st Century*, to an impending crisis – it is not a crisis borne of material issues such as we will run out of food or resources to feed a growing planet or the impending climate catastrophe – it is one related to something age-old – we have run out of narratives. Harari writes that our old stories are crumbling and "no new story has so far emerged" as we face a series of "unprecedented revolutions."[1] Humanity has reached a pause – not the end of history exactly but the end of an era when neat expectations concerning inevitable progress were baked in as it were to everyone and we could proceed with equipping students with more or less the same sets of tools as their parents and grandparents. It is clear to Harari that this set of beliefs and continuing to cram "information into kids' brains" is not the answer to preparing students for the next two-thirds of the 21st century. When information was in short supply a traditional remember-and-regurgitate approach to knowledge made a certain amount of sense – it no longer is fit for purpose. With information at our fingertips as close as our phones or even watches – we must try a different approach. The key skill they need is to make sense of all that oversupply of information. Making sense of that torrent of data requires more global understanding and critical thinking, what Kivunja refers to as the 4 C's – communication, collaboration, critical thinking and creativity.[2]

DOI: 10.4324/9781003123903-5

24 *Frameworks for Global Understanding*

During our brief lifetimes we absorb but a fraction of known human history stretching back 5,000 years or so. Most of us are content not to learn even two of the over 7,000 languages spoken and the stories of the people who speak them. The answer is that we form our understandings of the world we live in slowly over time and not all at once – we are mostly unaware of the process until we stub our toe on a news event or a fact that takes us out of our comfort zone such as a piece of a spacecraft that might come down anywhere or having to line up for gas because of a war in the Middle East or a ransomware attack, so the goal of the globally minded teacher is to help students reflect on this cornucopia of miscellaneous facts, views, myths and fictions and move from one level of global understanding – the one they come to the classroom with – to another higher level: what Robert Hanvey states in his essential essay as "An Attainable Global Perspective."

Hanvey conceived a global perspective not as a fixed intellectual capacity but as a "variable trait possessed in some form and degree by a population, with the precise character of that perspective determined by the specialized capacious, predispositions, and attitudes of the group's members." The writer argues that we all have different abilities to grasp parts of what it means to be globally aware and that if schools do not step in we basically cede the territory to the media that relies on myth, stereotypes and sensational visuals to create in people a worldview that distorts reality to make us more fearful of strangers, less willing to explore the enormous variation involving culture and belief across the planet and more certain that we do not have much to learn from the rest of the world. Hanvey argues a vital role of schools is to counter the media narrative that places groups in stereotypical boxes, for example all Chinese are conformists and Africa is a country, not the second largest and second most populous continent on the planet. Their role is to also assist students in acquiring the knowledge and skills they need to become effective global citizens. This is an often overlooked aspect of what makes global education different from most curriculum reform movements.

For Hanvey the job of the schools is clear – they may be as a corrective to the media's direction of attention to events:

> the schools must look beneath the apparent event at the phenomena really involved. If the media says, "Believe this way!" the schools must reveal that in other times and other places people believed and now believe in quite different ways.

The teachers' role is to help break habits of seeing and feeling what the media have inscribed deeply into our brains since childhood. To escape from the media's way of encoding experience we need to take a fresh look at reality – ask ourselves questions like, why are all villains in movies depicted as members of certain racial or ethnic groups? Why are women depicted in movies subservient to men – why are their careers less important? Why are terrorists always depicted as Middle Eastern and bearded? Why are protests always featured as violent? etc. etc. It takes a skillful teacher to challenge the prejudices that we inevitably walk around with and help students think for themselves. We cannot of course do this all at once but Hanvey points to a way forward by understanding that global awareness consists of at least five dimensions:

1. Perspective consciousness: the realization that an individual's view of the world is not universally shared and that others may have drastically different views. Just helping students to understand that they are members of privileged groups will help students understand people who support for example the Black Lives Matter movement. To do so is not to preach or indoctrinate but to point out the ways most societies allow whites to enjoy the mental freedom that neither they or their children will be the victims of police brutality and may get their voices heard in ways not open to others.
2. State of the planet awareness: an understanding of the current world conditions, including population growth, migration patterns, physical environment, economic circumstances of

various world regions, political developments, trends in technology, and international and intranational conflicts. Many students are unaware of some of the global realities. Wikipedia lists around 40 ongoing wars and conflicts with over 100 combat deaths in 2020 or 2021. Other important facts include that there are around 20 million refugees seeking places to live, and

> after steadily declining for a decade, world hunger is on the rise, affecting 8.9 percent of people globally. From 2018 to 2019, the number of undernourished people grew by 10 million, and there are nearly 60 million more undernourished people now than in 2014.[3]

3. Cross-cultural awareness: awareness of the diversity of norms and traditions of human societies around the world, and an elementary comprehension of how the ideas and values of our society might be viewed from other vantage points. As Hanvey memorably remarks, "Several million years of evolution seem to have produced in us a creature that does not easily recognize the members of its own species."

4. Knowledge of global dynamics: understanding of the workings of the world system and of the theories about global change. This is the area to explain climate change and explore what causes global warming and its consequences. The student who is knowledgeable about global dynamics will know the value of various alternatives – from stepped up use of nuclear power (using improved nuclear rod cooling systems) to the use of wind, solar and other fuel supplies. They will also know about the value of cutting back on the production of cattle, which exhale methane and use an untoward amount of water. In a world rapidly approaching a point of no return with regards to climate change, students must be prepared to debate, argue and use consumer boycotts and protest as necessary to make clear their preferences.

5. Awareness of human choices: recognition of the problems of choice facing individuals and nations as our knowledge of the global system increases. Hanvey insists in his own quiet way that the evolution of choice is a step change from a pre-global cognitive world. In the pre-global consciousness the consequences of our action "[tend] to be limited to the near, in time and social identity."

These categories are remarkable for at least three reasons: they were the first to begin to define the parameters of the field known as global education, and they suggest the way some students may understand and even gain some mastery of one or two of these dimensions and some may never develop and mature. One of the variables is the extent to which traveling and meeting people from other cultures will spark their imaginations and lead them to understand the world in a totally new light based on their personal encounters. Third, they continue to inform our current categorizations, most notably with regard to the 2018 PISA Global Assessment.

Quick Ways to Engage Students Using These Approaches

Perspective Consciousness

Ask students to bring in (print out) an article featuring a recent US current event that has captured world headlines – for example, a report of the presidential election and compare the reporting of that event in two or three non-US newspapers/media sources. Ask the question how does the coverage vary overall between the US and non-US media sources? How is it similar? What are the conclusions that might be worth drawing? Repeat as necessary to see if there are patterns that can be discerned.

State of the Planet Awareness

Ask groups of students to create a Jeopardy-like quiz show with categories that relate to the world situation. Each group chooses to write questions related to a specific category such as Languages, Rivers, Volcanoes, Oceans, War and Peace, etc. The object of the game is to challenge contestants/classmates to answer questions that relate to some remarkable facts about the world. Two groups of winners might then compete for an overall Jeopardy championship with questions posed by the losing groups.

Cross-Cultural Awareness

Ask groups of students to decide to arrange a virtual visit to another country and prepare their own guidebook as to five things that they can look forward to as being different from their own country with examples and five things that are similar.

Knowledge of Global Dynamics

Take three news items as reported by three different world news sources that illustrate some commonalities in the way the world works. For example there may be an exodus of people from one country that is causing a migration crisis in another, – or a way in which several countries are cooperating to share a vaccine as a response to a pandemic or a common emergency.

Awareness of Human Choices

Ask students to address a common problem – such as climate change, overuse of plastics or overdependence on carbon. Require groups to think of activities or projects that they and their future students could become engaged in to work toward a more peaceful, sustainable world, such as adopting a school in a developing country when they are ready to teach.

In 2018 the well-respected PISA test that represents the flagship product of OECD developed a global competence test "designed as a tool for policy makers, leaders, and teachers interested in nurturing global competence among young people worldwide". Twenty-seven countries or economies administered both the cognitive component of the test and the student survey module and an additional 39 administered just the survey. Not surprisingly perhaps teachers reported "a high need for training in areas such as teaching in multicultural and multilingual settings, teaching intercultural communication, and teaching about equity and diversity."[4] There was an acknowledgment that not all of what was valuable about global competence could be taught in schools. But schools, as Shleicher, the architect of the new PISA assessment states, can "encourage intercultural sensitivity and respect by encouraging students to engage in experiences that nurture an appreciation for diverse peoples, languages and cultures." The cognitive assessment asks students to "examine news articles about global issues; recognise outside influences on perspectives and worldviews; understand how to communicate with others in intercultural contexts; and identify and compare different courses of action to address global and intercultural issues." In other words how to practically engage with global issues – as they manifest themselves in the world. The PISA test provides a powerful case that teachers should strive to make their lessons both topical and relevant and that the habit of critical reading cannot be left to chance. Students must gain regular practice reviewing news items and discussing their global implications. Teachers must reserve this time which may seem not central to the lesson plan to enable students to exercise their critical intelligence muscles.

Pedagogical Perspectives 27

Figure 3.1 OECD dimensions of global competence

Hanvey's Global Dimension Categories Compared With OECD

OECD	Hanvey
Understand and appreciate the worldviews of others	Perspective consciousness
Examine local and global and intercultural significance	Knowledge of global dynamics
Engage in open, appropriate and effective interactions across cultures	Cross-cultural awareness
Take action for collective well-being and sustainable development	State of the planet awareness
	Awareness of human choices

Why Is It So Vital to Personalize Global Education and Make It Relevant to Student's Lives?

Hanvey tells us to go slowly and provides us with a road map for how to begin to unlock global awareness and consciousness for each of his five categories but his essay resembles more of a sketch than a finished portrait. Hanvey also wrote in a certain academic style that suggested he was quite removed from classroom realities. What was missing in the essay was how we begin in a more systematic way to apply these insights into the classroom. The real question for today's learners distracted by a media environment that is so all-encompassing is securing their engagement. To make global education work for the majority of students we have to find ways to personalize the curriculum. This is where we need to step back and understand that for any serious engagement with Hanvey's categories we need to understand that each of us has our own set of filters by which we see the world and those filters are in turn formed by our own social identities. In other words we all see the world through our own set of lenses. People born into minority families or who immigrated from one country to another have a head start on realizing the way dimensions like perspective consciousness and cross-cultural awareness work. Take for example Vice President Kamala Harris. Before she become the first female Vice President she began to understand growing up in a middle-class suburb of California as the daughter of two immigrants that her Indian and Jamaican heritage was being read as black and she intentionally chose to identify with that identity rather than as Indian-American, West Indian-American or Asian American. Like President Barack Obama before her who had a similar mixed racial heritage it is undeniable that the insights such an upbringing provided were vital to their success as highly empathetic people, not just as very successful politicians. If you had children of immigrants in your class the attainable global perspective could be much higher than without. They understand the different ways that they are seen under a variety of cultural lenses and can be extra sensitive to the ways some groups lack status while some carry around enormous privileges.

Why Is Starting With Experiential Learning so Crucial in Building Global Competence?

Recent research suggests that global competence development can be significantly enhanced through experiential education. That involves two kinds of student engagement – one that introduces students to real individuals from different cultures and which engages them in real situations that are relevant to their lives and to their global futures. That might include, as Barrett outlines:

1. Project work – these are common enough today with topic- or theme-based tasks suitable for various levels and ages, in which goals and content are negotiated by all participants, and learners create their own learning materials that they present and evaluate together.
2. Co-operative learning – in which students or participants do not simply work on unstructured tasks in pairs or small groups but work together on activities that have specific co-operative principles built into the very structure of the tasks.
3. Role plays, simulations and drama role play – simulation and drama activities in a foreign, second or native language and in literature classes or in non-formal educational settings can help develop learners' intercultural competence. For example, teachers or facilitators can give out role cards according to which learners have to act completely differently from their usual ways, norms and standards. In addition, they have to solve a problem, carry out a task or discuss an issue in groups following the norms of their assigned 'new identity.'
4. Theatre, poetry and creative writing – there are a lot of opportunities to inject alternative perspectives often rendered using a different tempo, metaphors and approach. Grappling with these new voices can be refreshing and give a new angle on our own literary canon.

5. Ethnographic tasks – these might include virtual field trips to remote regions of the world using Google maps, or interviewing experts over Skype can give students a strong and clear understanding of the diversity of the world.

We need to point out that the human need for self-esteem can be taken too far and can – when national rivalries spin out of control – lead to war that can sometimes be easily sparked by a nationalistic leader who understands the role that self-esteem plays in politics and in society. But conflict related to these social identities need not be the only outcome and here students can benefit from understanding how one more of Hanvey's global dimensions applies to them: cross-cultural awareness. In simple terms we can inhabit multiple identities – we can be supporters of the LA Dodgers, a Bostonian, Muslim and gay – depending on the context we can be one or all of them – but the important point is that none of those identities are fixed. In the words of Walt Whitman, we all "contain multitudes."

Enabling students to see that people can take on multiple identities according to place and context is a major step forward to realizing that attainable global perspective. Hanvey suggests that schools alone cannot accomplish the massive cognitive shift that will allow students not only to grasp identity as fluid but to see themselves as others see them and to recognize they have choices in shaping the world they want to see.

There are a few ways that societal institutions can assist. Studying abroad programs like the Peace Corps give young people the contact with other societies that is important to counter the prejudices, misconceptions and myths that the media was either consciously or unconsciously propagating. Direct contact means that students cannot escape from the kind of fellow feeling that occurs when human beings have the opportunity to socialize without fear and constraint. There are other ways to stimulate that global consciousness without students having to travel abroad.

One of the clear advantages of engaging in a global autobiography is that it may provide a purchase on one or more of these perspectives. Framing the issue using one of Hanvey's categories seems a clear way to begin in terms of knowing what topic and theme to focus on. For example, with a classroom composed of a significant number of students from immigrant families you might address the issue of how migration is discussed in the news. The idea that migration is a global phenomenon does two things – it depersonalizes their issues in the sense that it shows that migration is a global issue and that they can draw upon their own cultural resources to both understand some of the universal issues immigrants struggle with and use empathy as well as their cultural knowledge, including their first language.

While a standards-based curriculum may dictate a course of study to follow they rarely prescribe the approach taken or proscribe integrating that approach with other subject standards. The key is always how best to make the learning objectives – enhancing and enriching a topic so that the particular learning or knowledge 'sticks' enough so the students can apply that knowledge to solving problems seems to be the generic goal. But to become part of that student's understanding they often need a personal connection to the topic being addressed. That can be done through a local connection to their own town or community, age group or identification with an issue like global warming that manifested itself in a local historic storm, drought or hurricane. Those countries that performed better on PISA global competencies were those which invited in contacts with people from other countries. As the PISA report states,

> Significant and positive associations between having contact with people from other countries and students' attitudes and dispositions were observed in most countries and economies. The indices that were highly associated with contact with people from other countries are students' cognitive adaptability, self-efficacy regarding global issues and interest in learning about other cultures.

30 *Frameworks for Global Understanding*

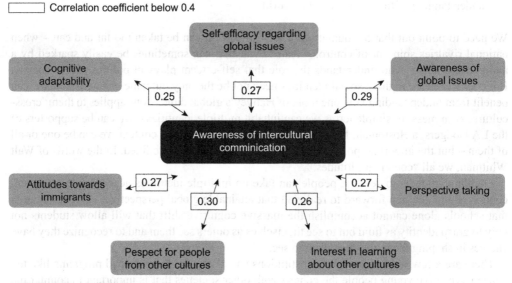

Figure 3.2 Correlations between awareness of intercultural communication and other indices

Meeting fellow students living in other parts of the world helps make the world real. In the 2018 OECD PISA analysis,

> the strongest correlations were between awareness of intercultural communication and respect for people from other cultures (correlation coefficient of 0.3) and students' awareness of global issues (correlation coefficient of 0.29). The weakest correlation was with students' index of cognitive adaptability (correlation coefficient of 0.25). This finding shows that students who have positive attitudes, such as respect towards people from other cultures, who are able to understand the perspectives of others and who exhibit higher levels of awareness and self-efficacy regarding global issues tend to have greater awareness of the nuances of intercultural communication multiperspectivity.[5]

The OECD diagram in Figure 3.2 helps to show the multidimensionality of what intercultural communication amounts to – everything from attitudes to 'others' as global awareness as well as the ability to be open and flexible in their thinking (cognitive adaptability), etc. Each of these traits are about even in importance so it is clear that one change in the students' environment – the arrival for example of an immigrant student or a racist attitude of an older adult – can radically alter the balance of this fragile ecosystem.

Quick Way to Get Started With a News Event

Divide the class into equal groups of students representing the continents/regions of the world. A class of 20 students divided into four groups of five students could represent Africa, Asia, Europe, the Americas and the Middle East. Each group will report on a news story for the region.

The news teams present the most critical current events of their continent/region. Each student presents the event from one of the five perspectives, making sure to mark the event on a map of the region and to provide updates throughout the week or month concerning the event's ramifications.

Follow-Up Activities Could Include

1. Each group sharing a documentary that illustrates Hanvey's five dimensions.
2. Each group focusing on one dimension and how it is meaningful in their local community.
3. Each group preparing their own short five-minute documentary about their news event.

How to Apply Global Education Concepts to the Curriculum

In the scheme of things global education is still a young whippersnapper – trying to find a way into the cracks of the curriculum. The phrase global education might be acceptable in academic circles and in faculty rooms but there is still a feeling that it does not quite belong in the curriculum. A curriculum is now more crowded with 'must cover' material and tests than ever before. As a result new teachers are typically given less latitude to shape their classroom, teaching approach and curriculum than their predecessors. My solution? Echo the slogan 'just do it' – if you picked up this book, you are halfway committed and hopefully by the time you finish it you are the whole way committed. As well as passion though you need to follow a disciplined framework – I adapted Project Zero's Framework for Thinking.[6] Global topics are not taught in the traditional manner – as you would history and geography. The content is less important than the process of refreshing perspectives and processing those of others. The critical thing in every lesson is to encourage dialogue and get used to finding a topic you can use where students can exchange their own lens with that of others. So the steps in order are to ask students to:

Lens for Understanding

- Think about how you see your world through what lens. Gender? Role in your family, social class, race ethnicity, nationality or region? Take five minutes to write down some quick notes
- Identify another person's lens and perspective. Pair up with a classmate and explore some key ways you see the world differently.
- Map the different perspectives on a wall chart as you consider your reactions to the case study/simulation or issues the class is discussing

If there is a low amount of diversity in the classroom, it is always possible for students to try on roles and imagine what the world looks like through other people's eyes. This can be particularly effective after reading a book like Toni Morrison's *The Bluest Eye* or a watching a play like Shakespeare's *Othello*.

Another recommended approach proposed by Veronica Boix-Mansilla is to use the three Whys:[7]

- Why might this topic matter to me?
- Why might it matter to people around me? (Family, friends, nation)
- Why might it matter to the world?

For some issues – such as climate change – it might be possible to pose a further set of questions around what they can contribute to a solution.

32 Frameworks for Global Understanding

- In my friendship group?
- In my neighborhood or community?
- In the world now and in the future?

As the Project Zero authors rightly argue, global dispositions are not something that you can just put on like a new T-shirt but need to be "extensively practiced" – routines such as trying on other lenses and reflecting on the different ways and engaging in the kind of structured dialogue outlined previously.

Frames

More or less any curriculum topic can be afforded a global frame of reference. Teachers are challenged to find the right frame and the Hanvey categories can assist teachers find that correct frame. For example if the topic at hand is the American Civil War – two of the best fits are perspective consciousness and cross-cultural awareness. Which ones fit best? A few ideas come to mind – how the American Civil War compares with other civil wars in history? How do other countries tell the story of the American Civil War? The OECD provides some further examples; for example a mathematics teacher might use the category of global dynamics to "invite students to decide whether linear or exponential functions best fit the data on world population growth" and a music teacher might take cross-cultural perspectives to "explore how today's hip hop is expressed differently around the world."

Case Studies

Case studies can be a wonderful way to get students engaged in global learning. They can appeal to the student who does not do well with theory and large concepts but can relate better to a particular example. Most commonly used in business schools (most famously Harvard that pioneered their use) they are now more commonly used in graduate education, particularly in the teaching of law and politics. But there is no reason why they cannot be adapted to the K-12 classroom setting. Case studies vary in type and scope – from setting up a real-world scenario and asking students to role play to looking at a variety of actual data that can be interpreted in a variety of ways depending on your global perspective. They can be given as individual assignments but a potentially greater educational benefit can be derived if the case study is assigned as a group project. This is because the best case studies invite a variety of 'solutions' and the discussion can bring these differences to light.

Next is a worked example of the kind of case study that might work for students in a social studies class.

What is the issue?	Nike has been accused of using child labor in the production of its soccer balls in Pakistan. Pakistan, despite possessing laws against child labor, continues to turn a blind eye. The use of child labor is also illegal under US law But GATT and WTO prohibits member nations, like the United States, from discriminating against the importation of goods made by children. Question: what action should be taken?
What is the learning objective?	Understand the global dynamics of world trade and the moral issues that relate to the unbalanced power relations between the West and the developing countries. Young people who purchase so many of these products need to be aware of these facts when they purchase their products. They need to develop as critical consumers.
Who are the decision makers?	US consumers, US Congress, Nike CEO, Nike shareholders

What is the problem's context?	Many western companies are using child labor or slave labor to make everything from T-shirts to phones. These products are some of the most popular products among young people.
What are the key facts?	Pakistan has a per-capita income of $1,900 per year – meaning that the typical person subsists on barely $5 per day. Is it a revelation – or a crime – that some parents willingly send their children off to work in a factory to survive? Is it cruel for Nike to give them the chance?
What are the alternative approaches?	Consumer boycott on all or some of Nike products Presidential or congressional action
Potential assignment	Letter to shareholders Letter to congressman/senator Social media campaign to boycott Nike
Resources	*ED Case Study: NIKE: Nike Shoes and Child Labor in Pakistan* *Nike's dilemma: Is doing the right thing wrong? A child labor dispute could eliminate 4,000 Pakistani jobs.* *In Pakistan, The World Capital of Soccer Ball Production* *UPDATE 1-Nike ends orders with Pakistan soccer ball maker* *Story-Branding by Empire Entrepreneurs: Nike, Child Labour, and Pakistan's Soccer Ball Industry.* Farzad, K. R. & Boje, D. M. 2008. *Journal of Small Business Entrepreneurship.*

Project-Based Learning

Like case studies, project-based learning provides students with a sense of control over their own learning as they follow their own interests. While case studies direct attention to a particular newsworthy item that relates to their own lives – for example Apple's use of Chinese factories that routinely abuse well-accepted labor laws, project-based learning works outwards to help students think about a problem they face in their communities. They work best when they address authentic problems that students might care about.

Project-Based Learning Skills

The following questions posed by the Alberta Department of Education:

Role	Journalist, storyteller, researcher?
Problem	What is the authentic problem, challenge or question the students will need to solve?
Research	What community resources and experts could your students use in addition to library materials?
Audience	How will your project involve an authentic audience?
Presentation	Performance, PowerPoint, video or combination?

Teachers often mistakenly presume that a project's final product, performance or service is the only thing they should assess, which leads them to assume that they should be able to tell whether the students learned what they needed to by looking at the final outcome. In fact, assessing what students know should be ongoing throughout the project. The end product or performance is the motivation for learning the material, but it does not necessarily demonstrate that they learned it all. The criteria used for formative assessment is the exact same criteria that should be used for final, or summative assessments. You may choose to give an exam that covers information or knowledge outcomes. Other summative assessments include: self-reflections, peer evaluations, or interviews. A thoughtful evaluation of the project is key. The final outcome is not the most important part of the project. There should be for example some room in the rubric for a formative assessment of the project with a question as to the extent that there was appropriate adjustment

34 *Frameworks for Global Understanding*

from the first draft so to speak to the final. Other questions have to do with the degree that the project was consistent with the challenge set out. For example, with reference to a challenge as to whether the building of an Amazon-like warehouse in the community was good or not for the community/environment, was there enough authoritative data presented? Did the students engage with a sample of people who might be affected by the building to know something about the environmental impact? Having students do their own self assessment of themselves and each other as far as how well their goals were met is good to build into any evaluation.

Travel Projects

Many people like to travel – students especially. Travel conjures up adventure, independence, excitement and a sense of escape from the ordinary burdens of being a student inside a boring classroom. You can send students on trips – by locating groups of students in a different geographical or even historical location. For example, you can break middle and high school students into teams and ask them to virtually visit a country of their choice and ask a variety of questions starting from the basics, such as which country they would prefer to live in and why, to which country is most advanced at reducing the pandemic threat and why. You can divide the project into three phases; in the preparatory phase students can use web and print resources to decide which country to study – they prepare a set of options based on their study of the people, economy, governmental structure, history, culture and values of the country. The second phase is to decide which country and to prepare a set of meetings that they would want to have with various people inside the country to gather information – these meetings can be set up as videoconference meetings or as email exchanges. The third phase is a vacation. They individually or collectively decide to plan a week's worth of visiting 'tourist' locations or plan trips that are just relaxing. In either case they are given a virtual budget – the equivalent of $1,000 dollars for example and have to decide how to spend that during that week.

Debates

There are lots of entry points for students to take up sides in many global issues that relate to the category Hanvey refers to as human choices. In his book *The Great Derangement*, the Bangladeshi writer Amitav Ghosh explores why the imminent threat and disastrous consequences of climate change are routinely ignored, suggesting that one of the reasons is simply the limits of human imagination. Another issue that lends itself to debate is the investment that nations have in preserving the status quo – those countries in the Global North in particular have no interest in disrupting the system that has always been run to their benefit. Citing some recent issues with regard to the cold shoulder the world showed to Syrian immigrants who were fleeing both civil war and climate change and the prospect that some 143 million more will flee their homes due to unexpected weather events by 2050, Ghosh fears that we are entering a period of the "politics of the armed lifeboat" where the poor of the Global South will be left to die in the kind of makeshift boats that Syrian refugees tried to use to escape their fate. So the questions for debate are the ones that have roiled the politics in Europe and the US – what exactly is the responsibility of the Global North to address what is clearly going to be an expanding set of crises. Some specific questions could be asked about some recent history – was Angela Merkel's decision in 2015 to open Germany's doors to more than 1.7 million asylum-seekers that year the right thing to do? To what extent does this offer us a way forward – the idea that the Global North does take some share of responsibility for not just the consequences of the Syrian civil war that it in large measure was responsible for but for future refugee crises that are likely to be much worse? While the decision moved many in Europe to the right and as part of an echo effect further motivated right-wing politicians like former President Trump to call for the closing of borders, the center just about held. Merkel survived the backlash despite it becoming clear that the absorption of so many refugees was not an easy process and five years later the German chancellor would leave the office on a high note.[8] Students are going to be the future citizens that will decide these issues – does the West support the armed lifeboat? Should it defend its standard of living by closing its borders to the impoverished or create special territories (as some countries like Australia and Greece started to do) where these refugees can be housed and live in perpetual refugee status?[9]

Amnesty International

Punishment Not Protection: Australia's Treatment of Refugees and Asylum Seekers in Papua New Guinea

In 2013, the Australian government took the extreme step of establishing offshore detention centers on the Pacific island nations of Papua New Guinea (PNG) and Nauru for people seeking asylum in Australia by boat. This Australian system is known as "offshore processing," and around 2,000 people are currently trapped within it.

In their prolonged detention, having suffered the trauma of witnessing violence in the camp and having been denied access to adequate healthcare, many asylum-seekers and refugees have seen their mental health sharply deteriorate. Around 88% of refugees are suffering from depressive or anxiety disorder and or post-traumatic stress disorder. Between August and October 2017, two people died in suspected suicides.

Assessment

Teachers might try to define in their own way how they would measure whether students achieve an attainable global perspective in one or all five dimensions. The OECD classifications are more teacher friendly.

OECD Dimensions	Objectives for grades 7–10	Potential Product or Outcome
Examine issues of local, global and cultural significance.	Students investigate where their clothes are made and under what conditions and circumstances they evolve from people gathering the raw material to their final destination in the retail store.	Design a presentation showing the route of one shirt or outfit from a location in a developing country to its retail destination.
Understand and appreciate the perspectives and worldviews of others.	Students engage in a conversation with another student from a different cultural background.	Write a reflective essay on the conversation and the insights gained from the conversation.
Engage in open, appropriate and effective interactions across cultures.	Students share a cultural event with others of a different culture – for example a Muslim prayer meeting or festival.	Write an essay or create a video or artifact that represents their effort to represent the experience.
Take action for collective well-being and sustainable development.	Students investigate the way their own school uses energy and water and provides suggestions (as appropriate) for more sustainable approaches.	Provide a presentation to the school principal and/or board concerning the way the school could become more sustainable in its use of resources.

36 *Frameworks for Global Understanding*

Each student should be in charge of their own portfolio of activities and make it stand out as a different kind of activity than the usual range of academic activities – teachers could award 'global citizen' certificates for completion of all four activities.

Before teachers do go out into the world of practice it would be a good idea to take advantage of grant-assisted work NAFSA completed that led to the *My Cultural Awareness Profile* (MyCAP). MyCAP is a tool that explores cultural context and understanding. There are many other tools that teachers can use for themselves and for their students on the Internet but the table compiled by the University of Michigan's Center for Research on Learning and Teaching (CLRT) provides a variety of competency-based rubrics that can be adapted to any project.

University of Michigan Center for Research on Learning and Teaching Has Listed Many of the Leading Cultural Competence Assessment Tools

- The *AAC&U Intercultural Knowledge and Competence Value Rubric* (PDF) was developed by teams of faculty representing colleges and universities across the United States. It identifies learning outcomes and fundamental criteria for each outcome: cultural awareness, verbal and nonverbal communication strategies, and attitudes of curiosity, openness and empathy.
- The *Global Perspectives Inventory* offers a self-reported way to measure an individual's global perspective in regards to the cognitive, intrapersonal and interpersonal dimensions of global learning and development. It also captures a person's views on the community and level of involvement in selected curricular and co-curricular activities.
- The *Intercultural Development Inventory* is a statistically reliable, cross-culturally valid measure of intercultural competence adapted from the Developmental Model of Intercultural Sensitivity. This instrument can generate an in-depth graphic profile of an individual's or group's predominant level of intercultural competence along with a detailed textual interpretation of that level of intercultural development and associated transitional issues.

After understanding where you and your students sit on the spectrum of global competency it is time to focus on your curriculum as a teacher and identify which topics, themes or lesson sequences lend themselves best to a global perspective. There is no golden path that can get you started on your journey – you just need to get started. The following represent possible gateways.

Conclusion: Why This Is Important

While at this moment there is a good deal of receptivity to the idea that students can benefit from global education – due primarily to the recognition of the impending severity of the climate crisis – if no action is taken we can, as others have pointed out, easily squander this opportunity. As Case makes clear, the "legitimate goals of global education" can easily be undermined when we have often commercially produced curriculum materials purporting to promote global understanding adopting

> a food-costumes-customs approach to other cultures that is, the study of other cultures is limited to relatively superficial features of their life-styles. . . . Simply teaching more about the world is not the solution – merely having more information may not advance students' *understanding*.[10]

We in other words must be more intentional in our approach. We cannot afford to pay lip service to the concept of global education and indulge in the warm and fuzzy feel we might derive from 'learning about other cultures.' That is not the goal. The goal must be to help move students along a spectrum whereby they can both understand more about the world's interdependence and identify a way that they want to be actors after understanding their own place in the world.

Notes

1. Harari, Y. (2018). *21 lessons for the 21st century*. New York: Spiegel and Grau, p. 187, p. 6
2. Kivunja, C. (2015). Exploring the pedagogical meaning and implications of the 4Cs "Super Skills" for the 21st century through Bruner's 5E lenses of knowledge construction to improve pedagogies of the new learning paradigm. *Creative Education*, *6*, 224–239. Retrieved from www.scirp.org/journal/cehttp://dx.doi.org/10.4236/ce.2015.62021
3. *Action Against Hunger*. Retrieved July 15, 2021, from www.actionagainsthunger.org/world-hunger-facts-statistics
4. Schleicher, A. (2017). Educating our youth to care about each other and the world. *OECD Education and Skills Today*, December 12, 2017. Retrieved from https://oecdedutoday.com/educating-our-youth-to-care-about-each-other-and-the-world/
5. PISA 2018 Results (Volume VI): "Are Students Ready to Thrive in an Interconnected World?" © OECD, p. 121.
6. Project Zero. *Lenses for dialog*. Retrieved July 2021, from https://pz.harvard.edu/sites/default/files/Lenses%20for%20Dialogue.pdf
7. How to be a global thinker. *Educational Leadership*, December 2016, Volume74, Number The Global-Ready Student, pp. 10–16. Retrieved from https://pz.harvard.edu/sites/default/files/Educational%20Leadership-The%20Global-Ready%20Student-How%20to%20Be%20a%20Global%20Thinker.pdf
8. Ofman, D., *Five years after migrant crisis, integration in Germany is succeeding, policy analyst says*. Retrieved from www.pri.org/stories/2020-08-31/five-years-after-migrant-crisis-integration-germany-succeeding-policy-analyst
9. For example with reference to Greece Europe's largest and most notorious refugee camp, located on the island of Lesvos – was one of the most population-dense refugee camps in the world, with 203,800 people per square kilometer in April 2020. See https://reliefweb.int/report/greece/issue-brief-blocked-every-pass-how-greece-s-policy-exclusion-harms-asylum-seekers-and and
10. Case, R. (1993). Key elements of a global perspective. *Social Education*, *57*(6), 318–325. 1993 National Council for the Social Studies. Retrieved from www.socialstudies.org/sites/default/files/publications/se/5706/570607.html

4 Ideological Framework

Conventional Framing

The Global North has a long history of bringing civilization to the globe. While it is agreed there were some dark sides to this history – most importantly, slavery – there were also many brave men and women who fought against it. The West has rejected its colonial past and sends massive amounts of aid money to the Global South. In various cultural and economic ways it seeking to come to terms with its history of exploitation.

Reframing

Although slavery has been abolished, its legacy lives on in the form of suppression of democratic forces, unequal trade policies and practices and support for dictatorial regimes, and despite recent efforts to correct the gaps in the way the story is told in history books and films, the West has not fully owned up to its unsavory past when it comes to dealings with the Global South.

Guiding Questions

1. Why is understanding colonialism from the perspective of the colonized a critical first step in global education?
2. How can we resist binary thinking by rediscovering the voices of the oppressed?
3. Why is it important to understand how caste systems function?
4. How should some of these concepts be applied to the classroom?

Why Is Understanding the Nature of Colonialism a Critical First Step in Teaching Global Education?

In shorthand terms there are two stories told about the world – one from the viewpoint of the developed/and for the most part colonialist world and those who were colonized. The colonialists' story goes like this – we were just interested in trade; merchants and the ocean navigators they supported wanted to find a faster trade route to the Indies and to China. As a result, courageous men sailing for God and country found the Americas and other lands by virtue of their navigational skill. Their courage allowed them also to defeat natives who refused to accept their inherent right to dispossess their lands and take what they saw as the spoils of victory which included the opening up of important trade routes between the developed and the developing world and the constructing of an empire that bestowed the great gifts of religion and civilization to illiterate peoples. This may be an oversimplified picture but it is largely the one most of us

DOI: 10.4324/9781003123903-6

Ideological Framework 39

grew up with in terms of the history books we read, the museums and the art galleries that we visited, full of the iconography of larger-than-life conquistador heroes, supplicant natives and intricate jewelry and clothes representing native craftsmanship. If you are privileged and white you see this as your heritage. If you or your peoples were on the receiving end of this conflict you see it all very differently; this was a violent and racist crime that was perpetuated on native peoples who first had to surrender their wealth and then their freedom to the white invader – those who were not killed by European diseases like smallpox were either killed or worked to death in mines or plantations. While this history was not hidden, the storytelling was so dotted with romance and fables such as the meeting of Pocahontas with John Smith or the encounters between Cortez and Montezuma the Aztec king, that the stories are to be almost read like fairy tales. Even Columbus's ignorance about his voyage's final destination in the Americas is seen as humorous. But despite understanding that the people he first saw were

> artless and generous with what they have, to such a degree as no one would believe but him who had seen it. Of anything they have, if it be asked for, they never say no, but do rather invite the person to accept it, and show as much lovingness as though they would give their hearts.

His first thought was to enslave them, writing in his journal on October 14, 1492, "with fifty men they can all be subjugated and made to do what is required of them." After his second voyage he sure enough went back to a consignment of natives to be sold as slaves. For those in the Global North offended by this picture of a rapacious class of white folk, many have been taught to believe that there were benefits to being colonized in the shape of schools, colleges and universities, laws, roads and democratic institutions. What gets too easily lost in this tale of western beneficence is that these were not altruistic contributions but were built to extend western interests. The people who were educated in the British, French or American schools would form the basis of a middle class that were sympathetic to the interests of the former colonial rulers and the elite would also attend western universities so they could become those countries' political leaders who would share the same values as the ruling class of the former colonial masters. We might also then be made to feel better that the West continues to ship billions of dollars to the less developed countries in the form of foreign aid that helps support healthcare and education programs. Philanthropists like the Gates Foundation have helped stamp out diseases in Africa such as smallpox and malaria, the World Bank provides loans for infrastructure development, etc. But the Global North continues to dominate the economies of the less developed nations and tilt the playing field so that the valuable mineral wealth in many of these developing countries that supply our modern electronics are purchased at bargain basement prices.

In other words, students' grasp on the history of colonization can be fragmented, which is not surprising since schools are taxpayer-funded institutions still largely telling the story of American exceptionalism, and every other country has its own form of national myth that offers excuses for racism and genocidal acts committed in many cases by some of its leading so-called patriots. The purpose of this chapter is to suggest to global educators that the history of colonialism is not dead and buried but because it has its roots also in racism against the 'other,' it is alive and well and surfaces again not just in American exceptionalism but into our student's present-day lives. The global teacher should be in the business of helping students see the way that these interlocking ideologies work and shape their worldviews.

We have to help our students see that when Columbus saw his first native Americans as kind selfless people and also wanted to enslave them he was acting out of human impulses. His sense of identity was formed just as ours is – as Hedges posits, "on what we are not, rather than what we are." As he goes on to argue, "we are continually creating in-groups and out-groups which pit 'us' against 'them.'[1]" Research shows that our minds are busy forming

40 *Frameworks for Global Understanding*

stereotypes of our in-group; negative stereotypes of our out-groups. Our in-group is honest, smart, upright, kind, brave, noble, and just; yet our out-group is dishonest, dumb, deceitful, unkind, cowardly, debased, and unjust. Study after study underlies the way that we imagine those we see as different from ourselves as being lesser, and at worst even subhuman. None of this is based on facts as such, but simply the way that we as humans imagine the world around us as a place of binaries."[2]

So our world is full of binary thinking. It has shaped our history and it continually informs the present which has been formed out of the binary thinking of the past. Why is this important? It is important as I shall explain in this chapter for several reasons:

1. Confronting the appalling costs of stereotyping.
2. Resisting binary thinking.
3. Understanding how caste systems work and the damage caused.
4. Overcoming the colonial legacy.

We began with a discussion of colonialism because I share the view with Wintersteiner et al. that "colonialism, still is neither perceived nor taught to the required extent in a way that corresponds to its historical and 'paradigmatic' significance." What these authors mean by colonialism still continues to dominate the ideologies and mindscapes of western civilization.[3] Colonialism is a civilizational reference point, a historical marker which helps us to understand the human and psychological costs of how our first attempts at globalization produced enormous suffering which continue to drive our politics and our relationships with one another. The next sections elaborate on just how this has happened and what we can do about it.

We cannot ignore our pasts. Those who do as the saying goes are condemned to repeat history's mistakes. Our global present is very much due to the worldwide western dominance achieved through some important geographical facts about the Global North, the growth of science and learning, as well as the institution of slavery. Our students need to understand not just the nuts and bolts about how the West came to dominate the world economies but the ways it has ended tragically for people and why. In an important but often overlooked essay, the philosopher and Holocaust survivor Theodore Adorno wrote in *Education after Auschwitz* in 1966 that "the premier demand upon all education is that Auschwitz not happen again." It's a major ambition and one that is not clear that our educational system can currently meet. Adorno writes that he[4]

cannot understand why it has been given so little concern until now. To justify it would be monstrous in the face of the monstrosity that took place. Yet the fact that one is so barely conscious of this demand and the questions it raises shows that the monstrosity has not penetrated people's minds deeply, itself a symptom of the continuing potential for its recurrence as far as peoples' conscious and unconscious is concerned. Every debate about the ideals of education is trivial and inconsequential compared to this single ideal: never again Auschwitz. It was the barbarism all education strives against. One speaks of the threat of a relapse into barbarism. But it is not a threat – Auschwitz was this relapse, and barbarism continues as long as the fundamental conditions that favored that relapse continue largely unchanged. That is the whole horror. The societal pressure bears down, although the danger remains invisible nowadays. It drives people toward the unspeakable, which culminated on a world-historical scale in Auschwitz.

Of course there are Holocaust studies and it has won a place on the K-12 curriculum but there is a need to connect the lessons of the Holocaust to modern-day events. In particular the Holocaust began with othering Jews. Othering as we have seen is a natural human tendency – a way to support the in-group against the group perceived to be outsiders. What is critical is how we can go from othering a group to so dehumanizing them that extermination and genocide is the desperate path taken by the in-group. As Hedges explains,

> the act of genocide while shocking, even almost unimaginably horrific, is unfortunately an aspect of human behaviour within a particular socialized context where violence is normalized, when the victims are sufficiently demonized and othered, such that their death counts for nothing, or more especially when their death is deemed an inherent good in and of itself.

In other words once a culture accepts and normalizes this behavior, we have the danger of genocide. Its clear beginnings appeared in Nazi Germany when politicians accepted violence of their supporters against those of other groups and then the politicians themselves incited racial violence and then passed laws to discriminate against the other. Othering can take place between minority groups such as Rwanda and Bosnia remind us. The Rohingya, a mostly Muslim minority who constitute one-third of the population in a region of Myanmar called Rakhine State are the latest victims of othering. For the Buddhist majority it makes no difference that they have been in the region since the 15th century, the Buddhist majority of the Rakhine State views them as "Bengali immigrants." Stripped of citizenship they are now targets for genocide. As the Canadian Museum for Human Rights reports,

> In 2012, violence broke out in Rakhine state, killing hundreds and displacing thousands of Rohingya. After an attack on a border post in 2016, in which police officers were killed by Rohingya fighters, Myanmar's military launched a crackdown. The military action, consisting of a wave of village burnings, murders and rapes, forced hundreds of thousands of Rohingya to flee to Bangladesh. Violence against Rohingya has escalated since then, leading to the acknowledgement of genocide-like crimes by the United Nations and the Canadian government in 2018.[5]

But easily overlooked in the process of othering is the denial of the vilified group's voice – they are not given an opportunity to speak to present their humanity or pain. Instead the range of vivid metaphors that can describe the group's low status is expanded – they are then referenced just by the metaphor – they are 'pests,' 'vermin,' criminals, etc.

So to address Adorno's view that the point of education is to avoid another genocide, we have to teach our children to recognize how othering works both in the playgrounds and unfortunately in our politics.

How to Resist Binary Thinking by Rediscovering the Voices of the Oppressed

If binary thinking is a natural human tendency – the normalization of the idea that one group – your own chosen group – has the monopoly on truth and wisdom and all the other virtues and the out-groups have no such claims, it follows then that schools need to fight hard against that tendency when it threatens to adversely impact other human lives. One of the keys to doing so is to let the voices of the other – typically the oppressed – be allowed to speak in your classroom. That means we need to hear from slaves, their slave narratives read in full as providing full proof that these people were not just Hollywood extras made to add some exotic color to the main story of white western heroism but real human beings with feelings. They contradict the slaveholders' claims that the slaves somehow enjoyed their lot. They must be read even though our normal tendency as teachers is to blot out the unpleasant and shocking but students as early as eighth grade need to understand the seriousness of the crimes that were perpetuated on the

42 *Frameworks for Global Understanding*

slaves including rape, torture and many kinds of verbal abuse. As one student states regarding an assignment that asked her to read slave narratives, as an African-American, "I took it so, so seriously." Studying and writing about what slaves did to avoid being killed or separated from their families made a big impression. "I learned what it was like to work in the fields, ten hours a day, with no food, even if you were pregnant," she says. "When they were auctioned, their mouths were opened and they were touched like they were not human, like pieces of meat." Nia believes that the harsh realities of slaves' lives should not be omitted: "Children should learn what really happened. They should know."[6]

Students should also know that slave narratives such as "The Interesting Narrative of the Life of O. Equiano, or G. Vassa, the African," had a global influence. When Thomas Clarkson read the work he immediately saw its potential to help his anti-slavery cause in England, and after a long campaign managed to get slavery made illegal in the British empire. Clarkson understood that his task was to humanize the slave – have people recognize the person as a brother, not some unholy underdeveloped monster. Equiano's narrative, along with suitcases of the tools, clothing and crafts made by Africans in their homelands, could show that these people were human beings with families. In order to awaken people's consciences Clarkson traveled an estimated 35,000 miles on horseback through the British countryside with a special traveling chest – he referred to it as his "campaign chest" – it contained "examples of iron shackles, leg irons and thumb screws used on African men, women and children as they were kidnapped, sold and transported to the Caribbean and the Americas."[7]

Excerpts from Olaudah Equiano's Autobiography

Description of Being Captured

One day, when all our people were gone to their work as usual, and only my dear sister and I were left to mind the house, two men and a woman got over our walls, and in a moment seized us both. My sister and I were separated and I ended up in the hands of a slave dealer who supplied the Atlantic slave ships. Six months later I found myself on board a slave ship. . . .

> . . . Thus was I like the hunted deer:
> – "Ev'ry leaf and ev'ry whisp'ring breath
> Convey'd a foe, and every foe a death."

Olaudah Equiano's Views on Slavery

Such a tendency has the slave-trade to debauch men's minds, and harden them to every feeling of humanity! For I will not suppose that the dealers in slaves are born worse than other men – No; it is the fatality of this mistaken avarice, that it corrupts the milk of human kindness and turns it into gall. And, had the pursuits of those men been different, they might have been as generous, as tender-hearted and just, as they are unfeeling, rapacious and cruel. Surely this traffic cannot be good, which spreads like a pestilence, and taints what it touches! which violates that first natural right of mankind, equality and independence, and gives one man dominion over his fellows which God could never intend! . . .

. . . Why do you use those instruments of torture? Are they fit to be applied by one rational being to another? And are ye not struck with shame and mortification, to see the partakers of your nature reduced so low? But, above all, are there no dangers attending

Ideological Framework   43

this mode of treatment? Are you not hourly in dread of an insurrection? Nor would it be surprising: for when. . . .

Description of the Middle Passage

At last, when the ship we were in had got in all her cargo, they made ready with many fearful noises, and we were all put under deck, so that we could not see how they managed the vessel.

The stench of the hold while we were on the coast was so intolerably loathsome, that it was dangerous to remain there for any time . . . some of us had been permitted to stay on the deck for the fresh air. But now that the whole ship's cargo were confined together, it became absolutely pestilential. The closeness of the place and the heat of the climate, added to the number of the ship, which was so crowded that each had scarcely room to turn himself, almost suffocated us . . .

This produced copious perspirations so that the air became unfit for respiration from a variety of loathsome smells, and brought on a sickness among the slaves, of which many died – thus falling victims of the improvident avarice, as I may call it, of their purchasers. This wretched situation was again aggravated by the galling of the chains, which now became insupportable, and the filth of the necessary tubs [toilets] into which the children often fell and were almost suffocated. The shrieks of the women and the groans of the dying rendered the whole a scene of horror almost inconceivable.

Happily perhaps for myself, I was soon reduced so low that it was necessary to keep me almost always on deck and from my extreme youth I was not put into fetters. In this situation I expected every hour to share the fate of my companions, some of whom were almost daily brought upon the deck at the point of death, which I began to hope would soon put an end to my miseries. Often did I think many of the inhabitants of the deep much more happy than myself. I envied them the freedom they enjoyed, and as often wished I could change my condition for theirs. Every circumstance I met with, served only to render my state more painful and heightened my apprehensions and my opinion of the cruelty of the whites.

It is not just slaves that need to be heard from but the many other oppressed people in the world – their voices are now available on YouTube as well as through blogs and other formats. Whenever people are being persecuted, whether it be in the former Soviet Union, China or other authoritarian regimes we need to keep in mind that their voices need to be heard. There are other more practical ways the global educator needs to take notice of this set of issues – it is that all groups, at least those represented in the class itself, need to have their own identities seen within history and their voices heard. Teachers need to know their students and understand that one of the reasons students get turned off from school is that they don't see their voices represented in the stories that are set out in the history books. It is clear that every nationality, every ethnicity had a role in the story of the building of the United States. Frank McCourt has a wonderful passage in his memoir about his days as a English teacher called _Teacher Man_ where he finds in an old store room some of the essays of former students who attended the school that included notebooks written by some of their grandparents in the Second World War. His ability to read to them their own families' exploits in the Second World War allowed a unique kind of bonding to take place – he had given importance to the voices of these students' families. They were no longer a random group of students without a sense of themselves or their identity – they had a history – a proud one of that of fighting in a world war – one in which freedom and democracy was at stake.

44   *Frameworks for Global Understanding*

Why Is It Important to Understand How Caste Systems Function?

Isabel Wilkerson in her most recent book *Caste* talks about the way that race in America is constructed. In a reference to the movie *The Matrix*, she argues the key to understanding America's master script is that "America has an unseen skeleton, a caste system that [is] central to its operation," she asserts. "Caste is the infrastructure of our divisions . . . [and] the subconscious code of instructions for maintaining, in our case, a four-hundred-year-old social order." Caste is the "underlying grammar" that can be used not just to understand American society but others as well where skin color plays a vital role in sorting which groups are awarded status, respect and opportunities to advance and which are not. Wilkerson shows the parallels to the Indian system in which enslaved Africans like Dalits were forbidden from learning to read and write and any chance of education or social mobility. It is instructive to know that the Nazis looked for inspiration to America when they constructed their racial laws as they saw that the US government had no compunction about stripping non-whites of their citizenship, classifying them as 'nationals' and adopting anti-miscegenation laws, which prohibited interracial marriages in 30 of 48 states – just as under the citizenship portion of the Nuremberg Laws they stripped Jewish Germans of their citizenship.

Globally minded teachers need to help students break the codes that operate – they can start by making some cross-cultural comparisons between cultural groups and understand how prejudice, tradition and fear all work hand in hand to victimize those in lower classes. Unless students know the way caste works, students will not be able to understand the multiple incidents that Wilkerson points to in which whites call the police when they see a black person opening their own mail outside their own homes or track a black man for being in the 'wrong' neighborhood. They need to understand the media's role which constantly reinforces the idea that blacks are inferior, not just in providing them stereotypical roles as gangsters and thugs in films and TV but disproportionately featuring African Americans when they discuss social ills like poverty and drug use when, according to the Kaiser Family Foundation, "the white poor outnumber the black poor considerably, 19 to 7.8 million. White people make up 42 percent of America's poor, black people about 28 percent."[8]

Deconstructing Colonialism

It is virtually impossible to trace the origins of racism and the caste system it fostered but colonialism was a large contributing factor. Colonial exploitation was in some large measure justified by racist beliefs and attitudes. Even after slavery was abolished (much later than the history books suggest) western powers continued to extract raw materials and gave them few resources in return for their exploitation. Colonial governments kept them from having representation that gave them any kind of political voice or control. In fact their history was rewritten to basically tell the story of how kind the white settlers were to bring 'civilization' to their countries. Whereas in fact they decimated them well after they first subjugated them. Not only establishing white racial rule in their countries but, as the British did in India, destroying native manufacturing industries.[9] So India and China were forced into poverty. In the case of China as Hickel relates, "Desperate to finance their growing trade deficit, they started selling opium grown in colonial India – on China's black market." When the Chinese resented their populations being sold an addictive drug the Chinese closed off the illicit trade. Not satisfied with this outcome, the British began the Opium Wars that the British won and then insisted as a price of victory that the Chinese hand over territory to European control so they could continue to sell unwanted manufactured goods to China and protect their own markets accordingly. China was forced to impoverish its people so that their economy "dwindled from 35 percent before the Opium wars to an all time low of just 7 percent." Their loss of control of their grain market as a result of European imperialism resulted

Ideological Framework 45

in famine as "30 million people perished needlessly of starvation during the 19th century." The weak notion that European colonization helped these highly 'backward countries' to develop is a complete myth. The reality is the reverse: these countries' living standards were ahead of the European as late as 1800 and in the South of India workers were paid more than their British counterparts. An even bleaker story can be told about much of Africa where colonial rulers like King Leopold from Belgium extracted rubber on such an industrial scale from the Congo that ten million people died under brutal slave conditions. You could say that somehow some sense of balance is now restored since these countries are now well on their way to becoming industrial superpowers but this is to ignore what happened to the smaller countries that were subjected to corporations that made cozy deals with dictators who repressed their peoples for commodities such as oil and sugar in return for keeping them in power. As Hickel notes,

> many leaders who crossed the west such as Allende in Chile, Mossadegh in Iran, Sukarno in Indonesia, Nkrumah in Ghana were assassinated by western governments or the victims of western engineered coups. Later they were controlled by massive debt programs as a result of the global oil price rise that subjected their populations to unconscionable levels of poverty as a condition of the lending. As these countries were forced to spend a larger percentage of their income on servicing the debt, let alone paying it down, social spending was cut and the countries plunged into more poverty, which in turn led to further deindustrialization even as the west was touting the benefits of free trade and touting progress.

It is important to reframe the narrative that arose quite naturally after the Second World War when the United States played a major role in forming the United Nations and helped put Europe, particularly a devastated Germany, back on its economic feet. The narrative in simplified terms was that the West was now a benign force in the world, not only uplifting Europe but the Global South. Truman's famous point four speech – in which he suggests that the failings of the Global South were all the product of a lack of technical sophistication and the West will now share this wealth of scientific knowledge that will relieve poverty – has proven in hindsight hopelessly naive. What was less naive and more disingenuous was Truman's belief that

> The old imperialism – exploitation for foreign profit – has no place in our plans. What we envisage is a program of development based on the concepts of democratic fair-dealing. All countries, including our own, will greatly benefit from a constructive program for the better use of the world's human and natural resources.

As Hickel describes it, Truman's statement was purely a public relations gesture designed to interrupt the flow of progressive ideas that were emerging in the post-colonial era.

Many of these countries in the Global South between around 1950–1970 were well on their way in preventing multinational corporations from plundering their natural resources and nationalizing industries before the West decided that such independence from their former colonial masters was unacceptable. A series of coups were organized to ensure that the right puppet leaders in Iran, Brazil, Guatemala, Chile and elsewhere were installed and democratic aspirations of the people they ruled were frustrated. Despite the brutal and deceptive ways that the West kept the leftward trends in check, the Global South found their way to express their dissatisfaction with the way economic progress was frustrated by unfair trade deals. It was then that the West found how to wield their power as creditors to govern the Global South in Hickel's terms "by remote control without the need for bloody interventions." Using phrases such as "structural adjustment," the Global South countries lost according to Hickel an average of $480 billion a year in potential GDP, sending many of these countries back into abject poverty.

46 *Frameworks for Global Understanding*

So it is important where we stop the clock. Historians are fond of saying that we cannot gain a really true historical perspective unless we view the past from the vantage point of a century or more. But doing so in this context renders our students without the framework they need to critically evaluate the past and particularly our relations with the Global South. If we stop the clock with the founding of the UN for example in 1948 or even take the story up to the freeing of Mandela in the 1980s then students are left without a real way to gauge the progress or lack of it with regard to the continued way the Global South is impoverished by the Global North.

How to Apply Some of These Concepts to the Classroom

There are several traps in teaching about the Global South. The first narrative is akin to an 'end of history' narrative that somehow the West has learned from its mistakes (or sins) and now we want to make amends. So we turn this tragic story of pillage and dispossession into a rescue narrative. In other words the West has confessed its sins and now is sincere in its intent to bring either development, democracy, freedom or all three to these stricken lands. The opposite impulse is that we in the West should stay out of the Global South affairs – period – and we have no right to criticize those in the Global South who want our standard of living, including our carbon heavy way of living and consuming. A third alternative acknowledges that while we have lost authority to lecture others about the right way to use resources, we should be prepared to look for genuine ways we can help to rectify the mistakes of the past. For example, we can point to our continued use of unfair trading practices, predatory loan rates and omission of voices from the Global South from multilateral organizations such as the IMF, the World Bank and the WTO. We need to highlight the fact that because of these practices, much of the Global South is impoverished As Hickel points out, we need to cancel at least $400 billion dollars in debt in 100 different countries simply so "that countries can meet the basic needs of their citizens."[10]

It is also important to point out that the past is contested space. As Orwell points out in *1984*, who controls the past controls the present. At this time we are engaged in reflecting on the great trauma of slavery and how we need to represent what some have referred to as America's original sin in our civic life. The Black Lives Matter movement has challenged the notion that those who fought the Civil War on behalf of slave owning should not have statues erected in their honor. Slavers in the UK who got rich off of slavery have similarly come under fire, and in one case a statute of a notable slave owner was thrown off a bridge in Bristol.

Globally aware teachers should be cognizant of all the teachable moments that the tearing down of a statute has vast potential to instruct. As the normally apolitical *National Geographic* remarks,[11]

> A major reconsideration of how the history of colonialization, slavery, and white supremacy is taught and viewed, especially through public art and memorials, is furiously underway. It grew out of social unrest and a tense reexamination of race relations that has raged since video emerged of George Floyd pinned to the ground and dying under the knee of a Minneapolis police officer on May 25, 2020. Calls for change started long before that awful encounter. Floyd's blood served as gasoline on a smoldering fire. (*African Americans have always fought for their rights – now the movement is global*.) Now, tough questions are being asked globally. What symbols from our past must be reconsidered or simply discarded? What stories demand a more complete and honest retelling? How should history be taught?

Students need to see both sides of the painful story – on one side those fearful that if you destroy statues you "sanitize our history, [and] . . . run the risk of forgetting how we've progressed and changed over time. . . . Those who come after us must understand that America was conceived in white supremacy and continues to suffer the consequences."

As opposed to former New Orleans Mayor Mitch Landrieu recounting in his memoir, *In The Shadow of Statues: A White Southerner Confronts History*, his decision to remove four Confederate monuments from his city in 2017. He called the decision an important step toward racial justice and healing.[12]

> Symbols matter. We use them in telling the stories of our past and who we are, and we choose them carefully. Once I learned the real history of these statues, I knew there was only one path forward, and that meant making straight what was crooked, making right what was wrong. It starts with telling the truth about the past.

Teachable Moment: International Debt Activity

Critical concept: How international debt functions to continue to demonstrate the power of the Global North over the Global South.

Key Readings

1. Assignments – in class, and homework assignment

    a. Simulations where players imagine that they are running a developing country but due to a steep decline in commodity prices (e.g. coffee) they cannot now pay their debt. Students role play the bankers, donors and leading nations to negotiate just how much they will be able to afford. Wild cards can consist of threats to join with other nations to default on the debt. Utilizing educational technologies currently available in most middle schools (computers with Internet connection), GlobalEd 2 situates students in a virtual, international decision-making environment focused on critical world issues. Across the country about 12–16 social studies classrooms participate in the simulation, each assigned a different country to represent. Within each classroom or country, students are further divided into a number of issue areas such as human rights, economic policies, environment and health. The students in these issue area groups then interact with their counterparts in other countries over a five-week period, through a web-based environment in order to negotiate some mutually agreeable resolution to a world issue like water scarcity or global climate change.

    b. Assignments designed to advocate, persuade other countries about the meaning of their debt and how it is affecting their lives.

    c. Exploring the colonial legacy – according to a CNN report many British stately homes are indelibly linked to brutal legacies of slavery and colonialism. And while their grim origins may have been previously overlooked, they're now facing a new level of scrutiny that – amid raging debates over how Britain reckons with its imperial past – has exploded into its own cultural conflict.

A new report into the matter by the National Trust, a heritage body created in 1895 to preserve places of natural beauty and historic interest across England, Wales and Northern Ireland, identifies one-third of its properties (93) that were built by the spoils of slavery and colonialism. What do we do about this?

48   *Frameworks for Global Understanding*

> The point of these activities is threefold – to remind students that we are still living in history – the history of Global South and North relationships are so soaked in the past that it is absurd to believe we can pretend that we can turn the page in any sense. Second, students need to experience what it's like to be in the shoes of a country located in the Global South – how different the world looks from the other perspective. Third, students need to be understand the modern tools of oppression (such as the lack of debt relief, trade unfairness, lack of power at the international negotiating table to change any of their situations) that now make life increasingly stressful for many in the Global South. In this instance and many others, we follow Mansilla and Gardner's suggestion that globalization should be approached pedagogically "as a phenomenon for exploration" (2007, p. 52) that examines a range of legitimate positions rather than employing narrow and fixed learning goals.

Rather than attempting to frame the discussion in terms of victims and winners and variations on that theme, a more productive approach might be to start where the students are. Research in this matter seems to suggest that they are as conflicted about globalization as the rest of us. One study indicates that "they held relatively stable narratives (or informal theories) that describe globalization as either a new guise for imperialism or as the foundation for positive interdependence."[13] What seems evident is that those students who have a wealth of knowledge and feelings about the subject, particularly those from distinct ethnic backgrounds, particularly first-generation immigrants, were more likely to find globalization negatively affecting their home cultures. One Turkish student, for example, who had frequently returned to her home country reflected,

> I think there are a lot of negatives to globalization personally because my dad's Turkish and I go to Turkey. Every year I go back and things change. I've been noticing that the kids are dressing differently. They started drinking coke and then they started doing a lot of things that my friends in America would do. And it kind of made me worried. Where is their culture that I used to love? I don't think it changed the roots of their culture, like their religion or anything, but I can still see more of the Westernized way of life in them.

It is the mixed bag – it is the teacher's job to help students make sense of it not in a dogmatic way but to show the way globalization is a continuation of a long encounter of the advanced countries (the Global North) and the Global South. So one instructional approach, the one taken for example by Bigelow and Peterson in *Rethinking Globalization: Teaching for Justice in an Unjust World*, is to lay bare the power imbalance in stark detail. The authors are aware that a legitimate criticism is that it is heavy handed and biased. Is it unfair or somehow biased to expose the realities of the global sweatshop industry, for example, our 21st-century poster children for the evils of globalization – the images of children as young as 6 years producing soccer balls Pakistan, and the abuses of factory workers turning out designer clothes in Honduras and Haiti? Bigelow and Peterson, anticipating the criticism argue back,

> Teaching is biased when it ignores multiple perspectives and does not allow interrogation of its own assumptions and propositions. Partisan teaching . . . invites diversity of opinion but does not lose sight of the aim . . . to alert students to global injustice, to seek explanations, and to encourage activism.
>
> (p. 5)

The authors continue, in a world where "vast inequalities of wealth yawn wider and wider" and "the earth is being consumed and polluted at a ferocious pace," then "for educators to feign neutrality is irresponsible." Thus, "the teacher who takes pride in never revealing his or her opinions" to students models for them moral apathy (p. 5).

The point is to let students develop their voices. They need to know that they participate in the global supply trade – their consumer choices, whether it is the purchase of a phone or a T-shirt, binds them inextricably to the global marketplace. They cannot feign neutrality, and together we can debate solutions and responses but silence is no longer an option.

Conclusion

The world is full of stories. Human beings are narrative-driven animals. We live out stories in our daily lives – stories of sacrifice, resistance and sometimes heroism. We tell such stories to not only ourselves but to those around us and we save some specially developed ones for our children. Since ideology also lives inside stories – what after all are socialist or capitalist or neoliberal versions of history but the selection of certain heroes and villains (the downtrodden laborer, the ruthless capitalist, etc.) – we are all subject to the spell of story making. There is nothing wrong with the human tendency to want to tell stories – the problem comes in not recognizing the story making elements and recognizing the way, like gravitational forces, facts and situations are made to fit a narrative. The one way out of this conundrum is to understand that we need multiple stories as much as we need to include multiple voices in their telling if we are to help our students transcend the traps that one narrative, usually an ideologically saturated one, sets for them.

Notes

1. Hedges, P. (2021). *Religious hatred: prejudice, islamophobia and antisemitism in global context.* Bloomsbury, p. 19.
2. Hedges, P. (2021). *Religious hatred prejudice, islamophobia, and antisemitism in global context.* London: Bloomsbury.
3. Wintersteiner, W. *Global citizenship education citizenship education for globalizing societies.* Retrieved from www.academia.edu/27646944/Global_Citizenship_Education_Citizenship_Education_for_Globalizing_Societies?email_work_card=view-paper
4. Adorno, T. (1966). Education after Auschwitz. In Henry W. Pickford (2005), *Interventions and catchwords.* Stanford University Press, p. 191.
5. Curle, C. *Us vs. them: The process of othering.* Canadian Museum for Human Rights. Retrieved July 19, 2021, https://humanrights.ca/story/us-vs-them-the-process-of-othering
6. Morehouse, L. *Engaging students with history: The power of slave narratives.* Middle school students connect with history by writing stories from a slave's perspective. Retrieved from www.edutopia.org/engaging-students-history-slave-narratives
7. Thomas Clarkson's campaign chest. Retrieved July 14, 2021, https://ageofrevolution.org/200-object/thomas-clarksons-campaign-chest/
8. Inequality.org. *Poverty more than a matter of black and white,* October 8, 2012. Retrieved from https://inequality.org/research/poverty-matter-black-white/
9. Hickel, J. (2018). *The divide: A brief guide to global inequality.* Windmill Books, p. 86.
10. Ibid., p. 245.
11. O'Neal, L., George Floyd's mother was not there, but he used her as a sacred invocation. *National Geographic.* Retrieved July 14, 2021, from www.nationalgeographic.com/history/article/george-floyds-mother-not-there-he-used-her-as-sacred-invocation; www.nationalgeographic.com/history/2020/06/confederate-monuments-fall-question-how-rewrite-history/
12. Landrieu, M. (2018). *In the shadow of statues: A white southerner confronts history.* Viking, New York: Penguin.
13. Myers, J. P. (2010). Exploring adolescents' thinking about globalization in an international education program. *Journal of Research in International Education, 9*(2).

5 Citizenship and Human Rights

Conventional Framing

Citizenship rights are only granted by the state. Human rights are an abstraction that relates only to extreme examples of state brutality against people who want to exercise their rights.

Reframing

Global teachers need to help students understand that we can hold dual citizenship of a global community as well as a national one. States according to the UN charter have a duty to guarantee human rights to their citizens and we all should stand as guarantors of those freedoms.

Guiding Questions

1. Why is cosmopolitanism a key element in making sense of global education?
2. What are the different varieties of global citizens?
3. Why should students be encouraged to exercise their role as global citizens/consumers?

Citizens now find themselves belonging to what Held (2001) calls "overlapping communities of fate": local, regional, national, international and, increasingly, virtual.[1] Our identities are now becoming more fluid – we are interested in a whole variety of groups that we had no idea existed prior to the Internet. From fan clubs of obscure bands, to followers of soccer teams to those who follow Star Trek or TV reality shows. Included among the trivia are human rights groups and social activists who care not just about rights incursions in their own countries but around the world. These changes provide opportunities for the development of new forms of inclusive democracy and democratic decision-making. This makes for a confusing world of clashing identities, diverse perspectives and, with the addition of social media-generated algorithms, ways to avoid reality as much as embrace its human complexity. It is no wonder that most teachers feel unprepared for this world or find easy entry points – we are all in some ways bewildered by coming to an authentic understanding of what global citizenship really means.

Out of over 700 teachers in England who rated education for global citizenship as important, very few were confident of their ability to teach it (Davies et al. in Yamashita, 2006). This finding is reflected in all other OECD countries. According to the Human Rights Watch, 71% of students interviewed had not heard of the Universal Declaration of Human Rights and 72% could not say where they originated from. The fact that the Universal Declaration of Human Rights (UDHR) applies to all the world's people and represents the best of the world's religious and philosophical

DOI: 10.4324/9781003123903-7

Citizenship and Human Rights 51

traditions is increasingly important as governments increasingly wrestle with domestic and international crises. To be an engaged global citizen you need to be aware that human rights despite the UDHR are always fragile and constantly in jeopardy. The hopeful news is that when you take the long arc of history viewpoint, there is some steady progress – from the rights of African Americans and women to vote, the progress against child marriage, child labor and slavery and torture. But there is no getting away from the fact that human rights are controversial, particularly following the 9/11 tragedy. The discussions of the attack on the World Trade Center and the Pentagon turned rapidly at least in the US. The attack was not seen universally as an opportunity to expand students' concepts of globalization, but rather discussion was unleashed as remarks of an 'ultra-patriotic hysteria' with predictable outcomes. The human rights violations that ensued (overlooking the fact that the US went to war with a country that had no connection with the 9/11 attack) in terms of the return of torture as a weapon of war and imprisonment of people without trial were normalized. As a result of these controversies we are left with only 15 states that contain the term globalization, and only two states include the term global citizen(ship) in their states' social studies curriculum standards.

Why Cosmopolitanism Is a Key Element in Making Sense of Global Education

To really understand the significance of the human rights debates a global teacher needs to come to grips with the cosmopolitan tradition. Cosmopolitanism suggests that the national boundaries and ethnic and racial differences are human-made fictions and are designed to obscure the fact

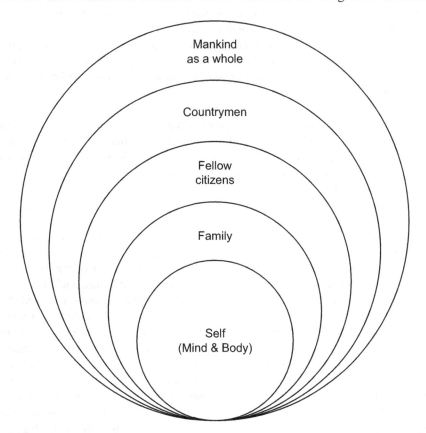

Figure 5.1 Hierocles Circles of Concern

52 *Frameworks for Global Understanding*

that we are essentially all human beings. The notion is encapsulated by Diogenes's famous reply when he said when asked where he was from that "he was a citizen of world." That famous retort needs to be understood and appreciated by students in all its radicalism. Diogenes became the unwitting founder of what became known as cosmopolitanism and an entire school of philosophers followed in his path. Students need to further appreciate how the cosmopolitan idea was refined by allied stoic philosophers to suggest that each human being as Hierocles states "dwells . . . in two communities – the local community of our birth, and the community of human argument and aspiration." So if you as a global teacher are looking for a place to start – start in Athens in 5 bc with this cranky old guy Diogenes or better yet his stoic friend Hierocles, the first person in history to imagine the human family as a series of circles.

The Greek Stoic philosopher Hierocles appears to have been the first person to imagine human relationships as circles. His words echo over the centuries,[2]

> For, in short, each of us is, as it were, circumscribed by many circles; some of which are less, but others larger, and some comprehend, but others are comprehended, according to the different and unequal habits with respect to each other. For the first, indeed, and most proximate circle is that which every one describes about his own mind as a centre, in which circle the body, and whatever is assumed for the sake of the body, are comprehended. For this is nearly the smallest circle, and almost touches the centre itself. The second from this, and which is at a greater distance from the centre, but comprehends the first circle, is that in which parents, brothers, wife, and children are arranged. The third circle from the centre is that which contains uncles and aunts, grandfathers and grandmothers, and the children of brothers and sisters. After this is the circle which comprehends the remaining relatives. Next to this is that which contains the common people, then that which comprehends those of the same tribe, afterwards that which contains the citizens; and then two other circles follow, one being the circle of those that dwell in the vicinity of the city, and the other, of those of the same province. But the outermost and greatest circle, and which comprehends all the other circles, is that of the whole human race.

The last sentence is the most meaningful and truly felt – it is a remarkable leap forward that the final circle embraces all of humanity and his understanding that our work as moral beings is to "pull those on the outer circles into the inner circles" and widen our circle of compassion. Even Cicero, arguably the leading political thinker of the Roman era, was influenced by the Greek stoics who took Hierocles's language and made it his own. Hierocles writes that "we live within a series of concentric circles that spread out from self to family to fellow city dwellers and then countrymen extending to fellowship with humanity." Our main task as citizens of the world is to "draw the circles somehow toward the center," making all human beings more like our fellow city dwellers. In one passage Cicero even goes as far to argue that "those who say we should think about the interests of our fellow citizens, but not those of foreigners, destroy the common society of the human race." For Cicero all human beings are deserving of 'dignitas,' including the right to be secure from invasion in the sanctuary of their own home. Plutarch, who was to write Cicero's biography, echoed these sentiments when he stated, "we should regard all human beings as our fellow citizens and neighbors." The famous stoic Roman playwright Seneca (d. ad 65) preferred to conceptualize "two communities": the one, which is great and truly common embracing gods and human beings, "in which we look neither to this corner nor to that, but measure the boundaries of our state by the sun"; the other, the one to which we have been assigned by the accident of our birth. There is a direct line from the stoics to the cosmopolitanism of Kant who writes a brilliant essay on peace that contains 14 points for the achievement, Article 13 – for example, everyone, Kant asserts, has the right to be treated with the same kind of regard to their human dignity as you would afford a citizen of that country. It is nonetheless a limited right:[3]

It is not the right to be a permanent visitor that one may demand. A special beneficent agreement would be needed in order to give an outsider a right to become a fellow inhabitant for a certain length of time. It is only a right of temporary sojourn, a right to associate, which all men have. They have it by virtue of their common possession of the surface of the earth, where, as a globe, they cannot infinitely disperse and hence must finally tolerate the presence of each other.

Kant in an extraordinary grasp of history links this right to not be enslaved or conquered by peoples who claim that they have a right above that of the native settlers to a country. Everyone has the same duty to be hospitable to the other and to the stranger.

The provision, although tightly drawn as "the right of a stranger not to be treated with hostility when he arrives on someone else's territory" has enormous consequences for the development of human rights law. Kant himself seems aware of the large global ramifications when he concludes the paragraph with the following uncharacteristically emotional summation,

> Since the narrower or wider community of the peoples of the earth has developed so far that a violation of rights in one place is felt throughout the world, the idea of a law of world citizenship is no high-flown or exaggerated notion. It is a supplement to the unwritten code of the civil and international law, indispensable for the maintenance of the public human rights and hence also of perpetual peace. One cannot flatter oneself into believing one can approach this peace except under the condition outlined here.

The language of the human rights community with respect to seeing a violation in one part of the world as connected with one everywhere is part of the essential DNA of the UN and fundamental to the Universal Declaration of Human Rights.

Citizen rights were thus understood as essential steps to independence from monarchies – such rights could only be expressed inside of nationally based republics. In this context the UDHR represents something of a breakthrough – to codify a universal and abstract theory of human rights independent of a nation state. The UN Charter's preamble begins "We the people."[4]

> We the people of the United Nations determined to safeguard future generations from such war which has twice in our lifetime inflicted on Humanity untold suffering, have decided to unite our forces for the maintenance of peace and international security, to assure, through the acceptation of the methods of this Charter, that armed force will not be used except in the common interest.

It is the only document in world history that references the planet's entire population. The step forward could only have been made in light of the Holocaust and the worldwide reaction to discovering its horrors but as early as January 1941, before the Holocaust had occurred, Eleanor Roosevelt (one of the leading architects of the UNDHR) was responding to the grim news from the European war. In her widely followed "My Day" column concerning the hope she held that following the war there would be a collective effort to bring about "justice for all, security in certain living standards, a recognition of the dignity and the right of an individual human being without regard to race, creed or color."[5] In that same month coincidentally enough, her husband FDR presented his vision for the future in his State of the Union Speech. The speech had gone through four drafts without any mention of the four freedoms; it made its appearance in quite a dramatic way, when his staff were suddenly called into his office because the president had an idea for a closing section.

54 *Frameworks for Global Understanding*

Why is this history important? Because we need to reaffirm that at the very beginning of civilization the bond that human beings have to each other was considered as foundational. Not just by ancient philosophers but later in the Bible in terms of the duties we owe to each other: "love thy neighbor" and the duty to care for the least among us. We need to be reminded of this in an age when it seems that politicians are more interested in making a point of focusing on our differences based on national origins.

What Are the Different Varieties of Global Citizens?

The issue of global citizenship is a concept that sits front and center of not only global education but at the forefront of many of today's most heated debates. This is not just because we are living in a highly polarized period in our politics with the right and left focused on issues like immigration and whether we are safe from perceived unchecked flows of refugees and migrants coming across our southern border and what is the status of children born in the US whose parents were not US citizens. Issues of who gets to claim citizenship, how citizenship is determined – through (to use the shorthand) blood or soil and how it is passed on by the mother, father or both – have all been live issues ever since nations became established in Biblical times. Rather than getting involved in these debates it might be more useful to expand on the different types of global citizens and allow students to consider the ways they feel they can align themselves to anyone of the following identifies that Westheimer and Kahne identify:[6]

1. Personally responsible citizen.
2. Participatory citizen.
3. Justice-oriented citizen.

The objective is to understand the entire spectrum of activities, not necessarily commit to one particular form of what might be called proto global citizenship. For the personally responsible citizen the objective is to engage in community activities that advance the idea that being a citizen is about giving back to society as much as it is a series of individual rights that the government must respect. So encouraging students to participate in activities like recycling programs, donating to food drives and cleaning up trash provides a student with a sense of community belonging, perhaps the first step to something we might refer to as "citizen consciousness," but this needs to be followed up by an understanding of what an individual contribution can mean by noticing the difference that community participation can make. The usual way this can be done is by setting an agreed-upon goal. For example, we will raise $500 to help feed the homeless this Thanksgiving. We will make 100 deliveries of food for the housebound. They also need to see the people and understand how their service has impacted them. A next step is to become a "participatory citizen" – based on understanding the needs that the government is not meeting and how citizen participation might assist. As the authors note, "Whereas the personally responsible citizen would contribute cans of food for the homeless, the participatory citizen might organize the food drive." Again it should not be a one off. There should be some follow up. What percentage of the total need was met? How might we keep such an event going year on year? What groups are needed to make that happen? The next level of citizen consciousness is perhaps the most challenging – it requires a critical ability to understand that citizens have a moral duty to advance the community to respond to changing social conditions. If they feel enraged about the number of homeless they might sponsor a petition or support a fund drive for a candidate who paces that issue high on their list of policy objectives. The justice-oriented citizen is the one that is fueled by a critical attitude regarding the inequalities they see in the society and will take action such as protest and demonstrate when they see injustice in terms of either threats to individual freedoms, or local or state budgets that deprive the homeless of funding.

There also seems a need for a kind of critical literacy regarding social activism that just buying the "right products" – whether it be environmentally approved detergent, cosmetics, fair-trade coffee or chocolate – is helpful but not really social activism. It can, as Bryan points out, be nonetheless helpful but she warns that there is a danger, maybe a trap, in presenting such "obedient activism," as an end goal, rather than as an "on-going commitment to social justice" (p. 273).

The Migrant Crisis: A Pathway to Understanding 21st-Century Human Rights

While there are some theoretical pathways to develop global citizenship, given the fragmentary opportunities that present themselves into the curriculum, opportunistic approaches to the challenge seem to suggest themselves. Teachers cannot ignore the massive humanitarian Syrian refugee crisis in which over a million refugees sought to escape their failed state. At the same time there was an influx of refugees from the Northern Triangle in Central America towards the US. Prior to that there was a wave of refugees who had been fleeing Myanmar. The story was hard to grasp in pieces – we saw the usual images of refugees fleeing their homes either in long caravans or in flimsy boats. The flood of images and information can render all these millions of human beings as faceless victims, or worse, as people trying to break into wealthy countries and draw benefits. It might be helpful to focus on one person's humanitarian impulse and what happened as a result of his efforts. Seán Binder is an Irish citizen and a maritime search and rescuer. In 2018 he volunteered as a coordinator of a Greek civilian rescue operation. Seán rescued scores of people from tiny dinghies where up to 40 people were clinging on for a boat designed for 12 people. Despite continued cooperation with the authorities, Seán was arrested for his humanitarian work and spent 106 days in pre-trial detention. The charges made against him include money laundering, espionage and assisting illegal smuggling networks. However, the real crime was saving lives. Human Rights Watch argued that "The prosecution seeks to criminalise saving lives." But not even Human Rights is revealing the real truth of why the Greek government is acting in such a punitive fashion. Facing 25 years imprisonment it was the Greek government's intention to curb the number of asylum seekers on the island of Lesbos where these asylum seekers are processed.[7] To fully understand the extent of the human rights violations in question, we need to return to Kant who, as we have discussed, first fully articulated the right to afford hospitality to the stranger that led to the establishment of the right in international law, more specifically Article 14(1) of the Universal Declaration of Human Rights (UDHR). Adopted in 1948, it guarantees people the right to seek and enjoy asylum in other countries. Subsequent regional human rights instruments have elaborated on this right, guaranteeing people the "right to seek and be granted asylum in a foreign territory, in accordance with the legislation of the state and international conventions." Later on this was encoded in the *1951 Convention Relating to the Status of Refugees* and its *1967 Optional Protocol Relating to the Status of Refugees.*[8]

Students need to know that the right of asylum was mainly created in the modern era to address the massive population disruptions caused by the Second World War and most notably the German persecution of Jews and other minorities from their homes. They also need to be aware that the modern crisis was caused by the Arab spring and partly by a breakdown in civil government in neighboring Iraq and Afghanistan. Over four million refugees left Syria for neighboring Turkey, Lebanon and as a result of the Syrian civil war that was indirectly a result of the US invasion of Iraq. When the Gulf Arab states stopped accepting refugees the only place that was left to flee to was Europe. This led to right-wing reaction to the notion of granting asylum to such large numbers of non-European refugees.

According to UNHCR at the end of 2019 there were 79.5 million forcibly displaced people worldwide with, according to Amnesty International, 26 million people of that amount being refugees. Students need to understand that as global citizens it is up to us to manage the ongoing crisis. Do we shut our borders like Hungary and increasingly the US want to, which leaves the world's wealthiest nations forcing just a few countries to bear the burden?

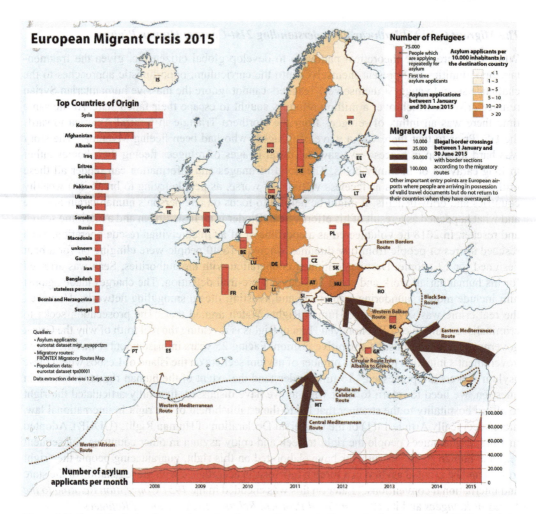

Figure 5.2 Graph depicting the number of asylum applications in Europe in the first half of 2015 and their routes of migrants to Europe

Source: https://en.wikipedia.org/wiki/File:Map_of_the_European_Migrant_Crisis_2015.png

Why Students Should Be Encouraged to Exercise Their Role as Global Citizens/Consumers

Students should understand their power as consumers to make informed moral and ethical choices about the way the world and in particular global capitalists conduct business. Put simply they can choose to support or not sweatshops, child slavery and unfair trade by selecting the products they buy. In prior years how these goods were manufactured was kept pretty much behind closed doors. Today with the advantage of the Internet as well as with international agreements requiring the disclosure of certain aspects of production to be printed on the label, young as well as old consumers are able to make more informed judgments about what they want to buy which often boils down to what labor and trade practices they wish to support. According to World Vision, in 2017, 152 million children ages 5 to 17 were engaged in child labor. Of these children "engaged in child labor in 2016, 4.3 million of those were in forced labor, and 73 million were in hazardous labor."[9] As the former UK prime minister has stated,[10]

> Child labor remains the moral equivalent of slavery in the twenty-first century. It is an affront to the values, laws and principles that bind together the community of nations. It is a violation of the letter and the spirit of the Universal Declaration of Human Rights and countless other treaties, conventions, and international legal instruments.[11]

Brown believes that global action is necessary to end what he calls "an indictment of their governments and the entire international community." But despite many governments expressing their intent to end the abomination it continues. While Brown is correct – it will take a full range of pressures to finally make headway against child labor – one lever that is underemphasized by Brown is the power of the informed younger consumer. As Brown writes, "More than six in ten younger consumers closely consider a company's ethical values and authenticity before buying their products." This represents a notable shift in consumer expectations of retailers. One critical element seems to have made the difference – the power of social media. Each brand now must have a Facebook and Instagram presence and that presence must signify some positive values. Social media campaigns can be effective as when pressure was put on the Starbucks to issue an apology following the arrest of two black customers for no other reason than they were black.[12] Students can be asked to critique the corporate side as well. To what extent, for example, is projecting a good global citizen image without reality? For example, what does 'strong action' mean when 'specific suppliers' are violating child labor laws? What are the 'root causes' that they believe they are tackling?

Understanding the Global Supply Chain

The rule of thumb is that the longer the supply chain, the more intermediary suppliers and manufacturers there are between you and the product, the more chance there will be some nefarious abuse among one or more of the intermediaries. An iPhone or a Samsung Galaxy depends on minute component parts, in particular cobalt, of which 60% comes from the Democratic Republic of the Congo where 7-year-olds toil under horrendous conditions to extract the precious metal. Students need to know that these mines are now the focus of a collection of lawsuits against Dell, Google, Apple and other makers of electronic devices that use cobalt and other minerals. The class action lawsuit was filed by International Rights Advocates on behalf of 14 anonymous plaintiffs (Doe plaintiffs), all guardians of children who were killed or maimed in tunnel or wall collapses while working in the mines. Consumers have until recently been kept ignorant of these realities – preferring not to think about issues to do with how many children or wasteful practices were used to produce the cheap clothes or plastics we all consume by the dozen these days. But as Israeli historian Noah Yuval Harari wrote, "A global world puts unprecedented pressure on our personal conduct and morality. Each of us is ensnared within numerous all-encompassing spiderwebs, which on one hand restrict our movements but on the other transmit our tiniest jiggle to faraway destinations." In other words everyone is morally implicated. We'll start with an excerpt from an article that appeared in the *Guardian*.

58 *Frameworks for Global Understanding*

Students need to grapple with the global supply chain – it's more like a global web that we all find ourselves in. So for example with regard to our must-have smartphones, there are several options the companies can pursue. They could:

1. Buy cobalt from other sources.
2. Force the mining companies into better labor practices that treat adult laborers better and leave the children out entirely.
3. Find alternatives to cobalt.

We on the other hand as consumers could

1. Stop buying smartphones if they contain cobalt from the DRC.
2. Pressure the companies to pressure the DRC to stop such inhuman labor practices.
3. Give up smartphones altogether.

After the students discuss the various options they might rule some out as impractical; for example the chances of putting pressure on the DRC might be considered limited since we are not dealing with a democracy. As argued,

> these companies aren't going to force anything on a company in the DRC. It's a sovereign nation with a police force, an army, and its own set of government officials. Even companies like Apple and Alphabet cannot control what happens inside that country. Does their money give them power? Of course, but that money won't overcome the idea that the market for cobalt goes beyond them, that the cobalt will sell to someone, and that the government of the DRC doesn't really care who buys the cobalt.

Students might gradually work their way around to a possible solution that might apply to all of these abuses. Corporations have two concerns – maintaining shareholder value and keeping their brand clean of illegality. As Lily Zheng writing in the *Harvard Business Review* points out, those corporations that abide by good Corporate Social Responsibility (CSR) principles are more profitable than those that don't.[13]

Students need to discuss how best they can play their role as global citizens to confront corporate greed and irresponsibility when it comes to the planet. What are our choices here? Do we have enough power as individuals, for example to boycott companies that refuse to act morally or ethically? To what extent do we have to act with and through NGOs such as the World Wild Life Fund and Save the Children? A reasonable aspiration would be to have students agree at least on a plan of action that makes sense to them. To move in this direction students need to be exposed to others who can offer examples of effective morally disciplined action. They need to be reminded that in some cultures the child is voiceless and supposed to work and not take school more seriously than helping to feed their families. They need to be reminded that they have the opportunity to speak for the voiceless and that the corporations fear looking morally bad in the eyes of the public and they will use legal and other means to silence opposition and hide information from the public view. As teachers we should do more than just acknowledge this fact that our consumer culture is growing to accept the fact that even if a product is affordable, popular or chic that should not overwhelm values such as if the product is good for the planet, such as helping to reduce global warming or contributing to a sustainable ecosystem.

One solution for this push back from the post-9/11 nationalistic wave is to try to play down the term 'global citizenship' and refer instead to 21st-century skills development. Fernando Reimers, along with the Asia Society, is a leading voice in arguing implementing a "comprehensive global curriculum with scope and sequence to run from K-16, with an emphasis on problem-based

Citizenship and Human Rights 59

learning, collaboration and innovation, language fluency, ethics, and social entrepreneurship."[14] Global citizenship is not a major concern in this framework but reappears again in OECD's Program for International Student Assessment (PISA), which defines global competency as a construct composed of three parts.

---

1. Knowledge and understanding of global issues as well as intercultural knowledge and understanding.
2. Skills, especially analytical and critical thinking.
3. Attitudes such as openness, global-mindedness, responsibility.

In contrast the NGO community, most notably represented by Oxfam in the UK, has insisted on using the term 'global citizen' in the late 1990s in their school curriculum activities, almost as a nudge for the UK government and others to include the subject within schools. As the NGO writes,

> Oxfam sees the global citizen as someone who: – is aware of the wider world and has a sense of their own role as a world citizen; – respects and values diversity; – has an understanding of how the world works; – is outraged by social injustice; – participates in the community at a range of levels, from the local to the global; – is willing to act to make the world a more equitable and sustainable place; and – takes responsibility for their actions.
>
> (Oxfam, 2006)

The trend among NGOs that have climate change as their theme is undeniably in the direction of students taking action, and as Doug Bourn argues, it is important that curriculum developers, because this is a rapidly changing area, "in cooperation with teachers and scholars, consider and discuss changes regarding the introduction of emerging social phenomena such as global citizenship." Bourn concludes that "we as educators have to make sure that our students will be prepared to become responsible and informed global citizens in the world of the future."[15]

Conclusion

Without an understanding of how human rights form the backbone of how we are all globally connected within a moral if not a legal web of mutuality, students will be lost when it comes to understanding such issues as immigration, right to asylum and the issues posed by the exploitation of labor. For students to even begin to understand the majesty of the Martin Luther King's phrase "injustice anywhere is a threat to justice everywhere," teachers need to be aware of the long history of how we as a human civilization began to conceptualize these mutual rights and responsibilities that connect us to one another and transcend those arbitrary barriers of states, particularly those with authoritarian tendencies.

Notes

1. Held, D. (2003). Cosmopolitanism: Globalisation tamed? *Review of International Studies, 29*, 469.
2. Quoted by Robertson, D. (2019). How to feel at home in the world. *Stoicism, Oikeiôsis, and Cosmopolitanism*, November 25, 2019. Retrieved July 12, 2021, from https://medium.com/stoicism-philosophy-as-a-way-of-life/oikei%C3%B4sis-how-to-feel-at-home-in-the-world-379be0252940
3. Kant, I. (1795). *Perpetual peace: A philosophical sketch*. Retrieved July 14, 2021, from www.mtholyoke.edu/acad/intrel/kant/kant1.htm

60 *Frameworks for Global Understanding*

4. United Nations Charter (full text). Retrieved July 14, 2021, from www.un.org/en/about-us/un-charter/full-text

5. Peters, L. (2015). *The United Nations: History and core ideas*. Palgrave, p. 138.

6. Westheimer, J., & Kahne, J. (2004). What kind of citizen? The politics of educating for democracy. *American Educational Research Journal, 41*(2), 237–269. *JSTOR*. Retrieved July 17, 2021, from www.jstor.org/stable/3699366

7. *Greece: Rescuers at sea face baseless accusations, prosecution seeks to criminalize saving lives*, November 5, 2018. Retrieved July 14, 2021, from www.hrw.org/news/2018/11/05/greece-rescuers-sea-face-baseless-accusations

8. International Judicial Center. *Asylum and the rights of refugees*. Retrieved from https://ijrcenter.org/refugee-law/

9. US Department of Labor, *Bureau of International Labor Affairs, Child Labor, Forced Labor & Human Trafficking*. Retrieved July 13, 2021, from www.dol.gov/agencies/ilab/our-work/child-forced-labor-trafficking

10. Ibid.

11. Brown, G., *Child labor & educational disadvantage – Breaking the link, building opportunity: A review by Gordon Brown*. Retrieved July 12, 2021, from https://gordonandsarahbrown.com/wp-content/uploads/2012/12/Child-Labour-US-English.pdf

12. Starbucks C. E. O., Apologizes After Arrests of 2 Black Men, *New York Times*. Retrieved April 15, 2018, from https://www.nytimes.com/2018/04/15/us/starbucks-philadelphia-black-men-arrest.htm

13. Zheng, L., *We're entering the age of corporate social justice*. Retrieved from https://hbr.org/2020/06/were-entering-the-age-of-corporate-social-justice

14. Miller, P. (2011). Global education – beyond "global lite". *Independent School*, 01459635, *71*(1).

15. Bourn, D., *Development education: Towards a re-conceptualisation*. Retrieved July 14, 2021, from www.scienceopen.com/document_file/d3a59fac-3a76-4283-aac0-3be0039ecc57/ScienceOpen/s2.pdf

Part Two

School and Classroom Approaches

6   Engaging in Global Popular Culture

Conventional Framing

The mass media (TV, cinema and social media) in all its forms presents a distraction at best to the teacher's work and should largely be ignored.

Reframing

The mass media is part of what students bring to school and can help us make sense of the way the world is experienced. For students to gain a deeper understanding of its potential they must become critical consumers of all its many forms.

Guiding Questions

1.   Why is global media literacy important?
2.   How do you grab and keep students' attention?
3.   What are some critical starting points?

Why Is Global Media Literacy Important?

Students inhabit a landscape full of endless global loops – their martial arts studio where they learn karate, kick boxing, or the latest versions of these ancient arts then present themselves as dominant themes in a series of movies featuring tough Asians taking down a relentless number of enemies. They can then re-enact their violent fantasies in video games available on their Xboxes or phones. The streets these fantasy characters roam could be anywhere or nowhere – we recognize the outlines of many of the same franchise stores from McDonalds, Kentucky Fried Chicken or Starbucks. The students could be located anywhere – Shanghai, Mumbai, Singapore, London, Paris or Bogota. They play these games in more or less identical rooms wearing the same blue jeans and the brand name sneakers furnished by corporate giants such as Nike and IKEA. So the first icebreaker so to speak is to ask your students (from 3rd to 12th grade) where they think a variety of things they wear or use are made.

Deconstructing Global Branding

Naomi Klein is one of the clearest thinkers about the way multinationals manipulate their image and seek to protect a planet-friendly picture of themselves. In her book *No Logo* she points out that Phil Knight, as CEO of Nike, was one of the first to make this association between marketing

DOI: 10.4324/9781003123903-9

64   *School and Classroom Approaches*

and lifestyle and made billions of dollars as a result of executing the idea to perfection by having the top sports stars wear his products and the Nike logo. Knight has stated that "one of the effects of branding is to make you feel as if you are part of a community." Our students live inside these communities and we might legitimately ask them what they look like – how do they differ around the world? One way to explore this topic is to again compare the advertising strategies for leading brands such as Nike and Adidas in different countries and the way they try to appeal to what have been defined as the "eight distinct teenage groups: preppies, jocks, snowboarder-surfers, rockers, heavy metals, hip-hops, technos and punk-followers." 5 A question teachers might explore is to what extent youth are happy to be members of the community that idealizes sports figures and provides them with mythical status through portraying them on ads or on oversized billboards looking superhuman or are they the victims of global branding? Does Nike's ability to 'sponsor' famous athletes lead young people to buy more expensive sports gear than they can truly afford so they can look cool among their friends? Is a sports shoe that retails for over $100 worth the cost of an admission ticket to a make-believe community?

You might share with the students their understanding of brands by beginning with a short story – about the way every Christmas an estimated 3.6 million Japanese families treat themselves to Kentucky Fried Chicken. This amazing tradition got its start when Takeshi Okawara, the manager of the first KFC in the country woke up shortly after he opened his first store in 1970 after he heard "a couple of foreigners in his store talk about how they missed having turkey for Christmas." Okawara believed that fried chicken could become the missing ingredient. As the BBC reports,

> It also helped that the stores dressed up the company mascot, the smiling white-haired Colonel Sanders, in Santa outfits. In a country that puts high value on its elders, the red satin-suited Sanders soon became a symbol of a holiday.[1]

Globalization hits consumers in surprising ways and marketers are ever ready to use associations related to the product country of origin to enhance the product's magic. For example, again with respect to Japan, Nestlé, the Swiss chocolate company, began selling a "whisky barrel aged" KitKat. An elaborate campaign was launched to entice consumers to enjoy the fact that "Its three layers of wafers were coated with chocolate made from 'rare cacao nibs' aged for 180 days in whisky barrels from the island of Islay – 'sacred ground' in Scotland for the drink."

KitKat has 'milked' its exotic UK connections since the product arrived on Japanese shores in the 1970s, as Gillian Tett reports – it was first sold as an exotic 'British' treat to consumers who were developing a taste for foreign travel.[2] Adverts in Japan showed "British people in distinctly British environments enjoying a KitKat break between action-packed activities," explained Philip Sugai, a business school professor in Japan, in a case study. "The message revolved around how Japanese people could enjoy life within the British context." But after a period of stable sales as Tett reports, "A trend had erupted among teenagers on the southern Japanese island of Kyushu when students between December and February. students had noticed that the word "KitKat" sounded like the Japanese phrase "kitto katsu" ("you will overcome"), so they were giving each other the bar as a good-luck token to get through the ordeal of juken. They subsequently modified the phrase to "Kitto sakura saku yo!" ("wishes come true!") in their Japanese adverts and targeted hotels next door to exam centers to distribute KitKats with this slogan on a postcard. The result? Thirty-four percent of Japanese teenagers told pollsters in January 2003 that a KitKat was their favorite good-luck charm, and when the tsunami hit the nuclear power plant in Fukushima in 2011, people sent KitKat boxes to reconstruction workers as a form of encouragement.[3]

The teacher can also point out that globalization does not flow from West to East but in both directions. Take the example of sushi. In the 1970s, Americans, according to Bestor, "rejected red-meat American fare in favor of healthy cuisine like rice, fish, and vegetables. The appeal of the high-concept aesthetics of Japanese design also helped to prepare the world for a sushi fad" (p. 15). Since the 1970s "sushi has become a dietary staple in most parts of the Western world." Formally dismissed as cat food, tuna now is a premium food thanks to Japan's "ability to transform trash into treasure around the world."[4] It was helped by the popularity of a TV show called "Shōgun," based on James Clavell's 1975 novel of the same name. The story, loosely based on historical events, featured a British sailor who became a political player in 17th-century Japan. Becoming a smash hit in the 1980s and watched by more than 30% of American households, it showcased Japanese culture in a way that was both appealing and exotic. As demand for sushi increased as Dupree writes, a worldwide trade in bluefin tuna emerged, transforming "fishing communities from Gloucester, Massachusetts, to coastal Croatia endangering the survival of the Blue Fish Tuna "resulting in an 80 percent drop in production and for prime tuna selling for over one million dollars at wholesale.[5]

As we have seen, the Black Lives Matter movement "became a rallying cry for minorities across the globe and George Floyd's death and his image traveling across social media became symbolic of all unjustified police actions. As Beckman writes, in the 30 days after Floyd's tragic death the rallying cry "I can't breathe" was mentioned more than 80 million times on Twitter, Facebook, Reddit and blogs, according to data collected by the Social Media Analytics Center at the University of Connecticut. The mentions "eclipsed brands that typically dominate social media conversations, such as Nike and Starbucks."[6]

What these stories suggest is that global brands are not monolithic; they do depend on the behavior of consumers and use the signals they send to direct their messages. In the social media world we are not just consumers we are actors as well who can express views that can be heard around the world; some resonate, some fall on deaf ears but the important point is that there is a conversational flow of ideas that ride the metaphorical global airwaves. The global educator needs to suggest to students that they occupy a certain critical space and they can choose whether they want to see themselves as victims of global branding or help to move conversations along. Put another way, students from whatever corner of the world they live in have something to talk about. This provides an ideal setting for teachers to engage in cross-country communication such as can be organized through a group like ePals.

How Can I Gain Student Attention and Keep It?

Global education demands that you engage students. It is not like other areas of the curriculum that tend to possess their own well-thumbed-through textbooks and are accepted ports of call – global education has no exam body dictating what content should be studied and how it should be assessed. This feature of course has advantages and disadvantages – the advantages clearly are that you can slot a global note pretty much anywhere in the curriculum and you have world news and topicality on your side. The disadvantages are that it takes some real thought to organize an entire lesson around a global theme and textbooks are often not at hand. But there is simply no excuse to ignore the fact that our students live on a planet that is both more interdependent and environmentally fragile than we ever thought and that with each passing day we recognize that the solutions we need to address our challenges are global, not national or local. There is enough time in the school day if we use it wisely. Most of the busy work we get our students to do is not productive – we all know what that is – stuff we give our students to do so we can relax for a bit and get our heads together. Filling out quizzes and surveys that we will never read, coloring in shapes and repetitive tasks. Global education is a way to wake up our students to some of the colder and harder realities of life faced by many of our seven billion or so fellow planetary travelers.

Grab them first with some of the things they care about – let's start with sneakers. They might not realize for example that Nikes outsources their work on their sports equipment to a variety of

66 *School and Classroom Approaches*

Asian manufacturers who employ migrant workers who come from all over China. Many of them are female and very young (between 18–25) and work 11 hours a day (in violation of applicable labor laws) in conditions that most of us would find appalling. As if this was bad enough they are forced to work overtime otherwise they suffer financial punishments.[7] The question is how do your students like their sneakers now? Such questioning can lead in a variety of directions depending on where you want to go:

1. Are all their favorite clothing and other consumer goods made under the same conditions? How do we know? Which ones abide by accepted labor practices?
2. What are you paying for exactly when you buy a Nike sneaker? Not so much for the labor it would seem so why are you being forced to pay top dollar prices for them? Are you just paying for the swoosh – the iconic brand – so they can pay the big stars who display their gear like LeBron and Federer? Are you condoning these labor practices when you purchase them? Or do you say that it's not your role to judge and walk away from the ethical problem?
3. How do you get Nike or any other global company to listen to your issues with their products?
4. How does it feel to be a worker in one of those factories? What choices do you have – is there any way out of poverty in rural areas of Asia? Is leaving a poverty-stricken rural village to make a few dollars working yourself to exhaustion the only viable choice?

If this lesson in global ethics does not capture their attention immediately, maybe the following will – SOS letters have been turning up regularly in western countries written by factory workers or prisoners who cry out for help. For example this is a report that first appeared in Vox magazine:

> When Christel Wallace found a piece of paper folded up at the bottom of her purse in March 2017, she threw it in the trash. She hadn't yet used the maroon bag, made by Walmart and purchased from one of its Arizona stores months ago.

But after a few minutes, she got curious. She took the paper out of the wastebasket, unfolding the sheet to reveal a message scrawled in Mandarin Chinese.[8]

Translated, it read:

> Inmates in China's Yingshan Prison work 14 hours a day and are not allowed to rest at noon. We have to work overtime until midnight. People are beaten for not finishing their work. There's no salt and oil in our meals. The boss pays 2,000 yuan every month for the prison to offer better food, but the food is all consumed by the prison guards. Sick inmates have to pay for their own pills. Prisons in China cannot be compared to prisons in the United States. Horse, cow, goat, pig, dog.

After extensive checking, Walmart issued its statement about there being "no way to verify the origin of the letter," but after the company launched an internal investigation. It was found that the factory that made the

> purse didn't adhere to Walmart's standards, which stress the need for "labor to be voluntary" and state that "slave, child, underage, forced, bonded, or indentured labor will not be tolerated." As a result, the company cut ties with the supplier, a decision the company only disclosed after it was contacted for this story. Walmart declined to clarify whether the supplier in question had contracted with Yingshan prison.

It is these types of stories that can and should catch students' attention[9] and again the discussion can go in many different directions. The essential question is what price are we prepared to pay

Engaging in Global Popular Culture   67

Table 6.1 Follow-up activity: price of western consumerism

1. Read the interview with Jim Keady, a soccer coach who filmed the documentary *Behind the Swoosh* and judge for yourself the ethics of producing shoes where a fraction of the price of the shoe ($1–$2) goes to workers who have to live in primitive prison conditions so that Tiger Woods can earn in one second (through Nike sponsorship) the cost of a house for one of these workers. In the summer of 2000 Keady went to live in Indonesia and worked at a Nike sweatshop:

   > I tried to survive on the wages they get paid. In one month, I lost 25 pounds. you're making about $100 a month. Your rent, your drinking water and any transportation is going to cost you, collectively, about 500,000 rubia. You're left with 500,050 rubia for the rest of the month. . . . What about food? What about clothes? What about modest recreation? . . . A Coke is 3,000 rubia. A kilo of bananas is 8,000.

   (http://vimeo.com/6109896)

2. Review Jim Keady's documentary which contains an interview with Phil Knight. Nike argues that it is supplying much-needed jobs in emerging countries like Indonesia and if people do not want them they are free to leave. They also claim that they have begun monitoring the factories and instituting some labor standards (see the Wikipedia article on Nike Sweatshops http://en.wikipedia.org/wiki/Nike_sweatshops). Advocates for Nike can also reference their support of women's sports which took off in the 1990s after Nike began to provide endorsement money for some top female athletes.
3. Imagine you are a sports team whom Nike regularly sponsors. Fans are asking questions about what you are going to do with regard to continuing to be sponsored in light of these trading practices. In groups write a statement declaring your future policy.
4. Who are the major brand ambassadors of Nike? Write a letter to one of them and express your feelings as to whether or not they should continue to support the brand.
5. Discuss the question concerning whether a genuine youth culture exists apart from the way a youth culture is sold to youth by corporations. What are the ways that young people in the US and in a selected country – possibly the country you have chosen to partner with through ePals – have resisted the global marketing efforts?

to acquire cheap goods? What is the true price of fashion? What is the true price of modern-day consumer choice?

What Are the Conceptual Barriers Students Need to Overcome?

Once you have your students' attention through a pocketbook issue such as what price they are prepared to pay for their consumer choices, then where do you take their interest? You might go on to explore the world of sports and entertainment and have your students discover for themselves why salaries between women's and men's sports vary so widely. Or how the team's global merchandising of everything from shirts to bobbleheads follows the selling of international cable rights. Getting these concepts and grasping the global nature of nearly everything that touches them are valuable but tend not to generate really profound insights. Students in other words need to be encouraged to go deeper.

Hanvey, writing from the relatively placid media world of the 1970s in his highly influential essay *An Attainable Global Perspective*, suggests that the globally minded teacher is constantly in a hidden dialogue with the media. The anthropologist forcefully argues that the schools cannot avoid their responsibility to help their students engage in its various distortions: "schools must stake out a niche that balances and corrects the media. The schools may be bearers of culture but they are also agents of an academic tradition that encourages scrutiny of that which seems conventional and obvious." So you grab the students' attention by not ignoring the media but using some of the issues it raises as curriculum. Despite the multiple news outlets that students have access to on their computers and mobile devices – most are according to current surveys painfully ignorant of the world's realities.[10]

68 *School and Classroom Approaches*

- Eighty-five percent of 18- to 24-year-old Americans were unable to locate Afghanistan and Iraq on a map in a 2002 National Geographic Society survey despite the fact the US was at war or publicly preparing for war in both countries.
- Sixty-nine percent were unable to locate Great Britain and 29% were unable to find the Pacific Ocean.

The lack of basic knowledge about the world is related to the fact that most teachers have given them no reason to feel connected or believe that non-US locations have value or meaning. Yes many have retired into their own media cocoon – we also know that the major networks have seen a decline in their viewership, so the 7 pm news bulletin that used to provide a sense of authority to the selection of news stories is no longer. Teachers must fill the vacuum and introduce discussions about the news as they explore topics in social studies most directly but also in science and in teaching foreign languages. Students' global literary scores will rise if they see these issues are important to the adults in their lives who most notably are teachers. If you don't get into the habit of analyzing information from a global perspective you end up with some very distressing outcomes such as the results of a recent US state survey that found that "almost two-thirds of young American adults did not know that 6 million Jews were killed during the Holocaust, and more than one in 10 believe Jews caused the Holocaust," The same *Guardian* report from which these statistics were derived also reported that

> almost a quarter of respondents (23%) said they believed the Holocaust was a myth, or had been exaggerated, or they weren't sure. One in eight (12%) said they had definitely not heard, or didn't think they had heard, about the Holocaust.[11]

Students need to be engaged in understanding the complex world where KFC and McDonald's franchises thrive in the Muslim world. The question is how to begin. One initial step might be to become better, more informed consumers. Students today, unlike any generation before them, use consumer choices to express their personal identity. Those selling everything from electric cars to toasters know this and through their branding messages are able to capitalize on this knowledge. The question is are students going to be manipulated by these messages or are they going to be able to form independent judgments so that they can sort out fake environmentally friendly companies from the real thing. They need to know how companies are increasingly using social media to influence their young online consumers who can now press a button on their mobile phone to purchase an item. A review of TikTok and viral YouTube videos will reveal an interesting tension between those who are subtly able to insert a commercial in their production and those that want to keep their art pure from such contamination. Students might be encouraged to make a list of the more effective social media-produced product pitches and those that are not quite as successful. There are other conceptual challenges that the teacher must work hard to address. Among them include the tendency we all have, as does the media in spades, to stereotype people based on national and supposedly ethnic characteristics. So our challenges are the following.

Busting Open Stereotyping Myths

We are taught to see the world through a particular cultural frame – it begins with our films and our reading and ends up as being processed as normal. Think of any movie – how often is the bad character a foreigner who speaks with broken English? In Bond movies, 007 opponents are East Europeans in suits and if they are female they are seductresses. Chinese characters are depicted as described later – during the 1960s as oddly sinister, members of the underworld and today they are what are considered to be a 'model minority.'

Stereotype Busting

A good first step in stereotype busting is to have students write down what they think when a place or a person comes to mind. So suppose you wrote up on the board the word Africa and asked what images or ideas come to mind. Lions, jungles, diamonds and a whole lot of highly evocative Hollywood-inspired thoughts are likely to come to mind. The follow-up should be some activities designed to counter these stereotypes. You can start with the fact that Africa is a continent and not a country. Its 54 countries form the second largest continental land mass next to Asia spanning 11.6 million square miles with an estimated population of 1.3 billion. Students might visit on the web photos of modern-day Johannesburg with 4.4 million inhabitants and Lagos, Nigeria, with five times that amount of people and the seventh largest economy in Africa.

To counter their stereotypes, the teacher can provide the human dimension by connecting their classroom to a variety of cultural websites that enable them to visit children in other countries. There are plenty of resources provided by sites like Oxfam and iEARN. These groups mange platforms that allow classrooms to connect directly so they can work on projects around the globe.

A similar chart could be composed for Muslims and Arabs who are often depicted in the media in a similarly negative way – they are often typecast as terrorists, prone to violent temper and constantly seeking revenge. Most of the time we ignore the way popular culture has already shaped our students' perceptions and we continue to teach without regard to biases that have nested in their brain subconsciously. They often lie dormant in our brain, waiting to be reconfirmed by the next movie or in some cases the next irresponsible politician wanting to justify an exclusionary or discriminatory policy such as a ban on all Muslims. If we don't engage with these realities we risk missing our students' real thinking – if we simply try to pump inert information about cultures that make them seem pure and unrelated to current perceptions then we risk irrelevance. What we should do in the classroom is encourage critical thinking – to ask why these kinds of stereotypes exist and continue to dominate popular culture and to ask why the remnants of the colonial views of once colonized peoples and cultures can still be detected in everything from textbooks to advertisements.

As stated, "the truth is that digital literacy is a messy topography." As Lankshear and Knobel (2008) reflect, "the most immediately obvious facts about accounts of digital literacy are that there are many of them and that there are significantly different *kinds* of concepts on offer."[12]

Critical Stereotyping-Busting Activities from Merry Merryfield

American students often come to school believing many stereotypes or misinformation about people in other regions of the world. Recently, I visited a third grade classroom where the teacher was beginning a unit in South Africa. She began by asking, "What do you know about South Africa?" The students' hands shot up and their replies were grouped on the board into these generalities: there are lots of wild animals; people don't wear clothes or live in houses; it is jungle/hot, people are starving/poor. When she asked them, "Why would you like to visit South Africa?" over 80% of the responses were related to seeing wild animals. Other responses focused on seeing people who eat bugs, carry spears, play drums, etc.

70　*School and Classroom Approaches*

To counter their stereotypes, the teacher provided the students with activities that addressed their misperceptions. The students worked with visuals of diverse South African families and their homes in rural and urban communities in the 1980s and today, vegetation and climate maps (no "jungles!" the students were amazed to discover), a video shown by tourists visiting animals in game parks, and menus from some restaurants in Durban and Cape Town. The students also visited websites of some South African elementary schools and looked at some sections of online South African newspapers.1 They compared *Journey to Jo'burg* with *The Day Gogo Went to Vote* to learn about apartheid, economic inequities and political change in South African children's lives, and then discussed the books with two South African students who were attending a local university. By the end of the unit, the students had identified many commonalities that they shared with South Africans and understood the danger of stereotypes and exotic images.

Recognizing Your Own Privilege

Students need to face up to two facts about their lives that they are probably not aware of: first for the white students to recognize their own privilege and the way that privilege is hard won at the expense of a mass of people who are struggling to survive. Second, they need to understand that if they live in the privileged West their countries' wealth and power is derived in part from exploitative relations with the Global South. The great philosopher and exponent of cosmo-politanism Martha Nussbaum believes that you cannot view yourself as fully educated unless you can look at yourself and your culture from the outside. "Through cross-cultural inquiry," Nussbaum maintains,

> students may realize that what they have taken to be natural and normal – and therefore what they are most comfortable with – is merely parochial and habitual. Fostering a greater knowledge of the world and its peoples will develop students who can operate as world citizens with greater sensitivity and understanding.

The reason to do so is not always clear to people mired in a nation-centric perspective – it is as Nussbaum eloquently argues for educational reasons – we see ourselves more clearly and can solve many more problems when we enter into the minds of others. It forces us to step out of the often dangerous prejudice that our own country represents the summit of civilized thought and that others' shortcomings can be explained by the accident that they were born in another country. As Nussbaum reminds us, stoic values may not be readily apparent in terms of the way the world is governed nowadays but they have inscribed themselves deeply into our core beliefs – most notably our respect for everyone's right to human dignity and freedom to pursue happiness.

Detecting 'Greenwashing'

Large and small corporations recognize the appeal of being green – whether it be the growing of organic produce or being earth friendly, which usually means using environmentally friendly ingredients in the manufacture of products. Greenwashing is a form of media manipulation designed to add value to their brand by pretending to be something they are not. BP is a case in point. As Ethical Consumer points out, BP projects a "keen focus on investing in environment-friendly energy (but) the fact remains that 96% of their annual capital expenditure is spent on non-renewable oil and gas. Going by their own figures, BP is investing $500 million a year in low-carbon initiatives, less than 4% of overall investment."[13]

Engaging in Global Popular Culture   71

There are, as Ethical Consumer explains, many other companies that engage in similar deceptive practices. The NGO offers a critical guide on how to tell if a company is greenwashing.

Conclusion

Students inhabit a world that is now so saturated with media messages that are obtainable not just at the click of a phone but called up every time they turn on a TV or visit a gas station or supermarket. We cannot escape from the fact that these images, created in many cases by global multinationals, have influenced students deeply whether they are aware of it or not. One of the teachers' roles is to tease out their deep structures. The problem comes when some 'media messages' may tell stories that are not by themselves inaccurate but are nevertheless fundamentally dishonest because they play on age-old narratives related to their brand image as on the 'side of the environment,' science and medicine or 'family values.' Decoding some of these messages takes a lot more effort than most of us have time for but make the effort we must. If we give students the ability to deconstruct just one misleading ad they will have the tools to unlock many more for themselves.

Notes

1. Barton, E. (2016). Why Japan celebrates Christmas with KFC. *BBC, Japan*, December 19. Retrieved July 17, 2021, from www.bbc.com/worklife/article/20161216-why-japan-celebrates-christmas-with-kfc
2. Tett, G., How the KitKat went global. *Financial Times*. Retrieved July 17, 2021, from www.ft.com/content/7ec44105-c123-4dc8-a262-e5747eae1e1a
3. Ibid.
4. Geezer (2012). *The latest victims of innovation*, February, 21. Retrieved from http://controversyandhyperbole.blogspot.com/2012/02/what-fuck-or-how-sushi-went-global.html
5. Bland, A. (2013). *From cat food to sushi counter: The strange rise of the bluefin tuna*, September, 11. Retrieved from www.smithsonianmag.com/arts-culture/from-cat-food-to-sushi-counter-the-strange-rise-of-the-bluefin-tuna-5980010/
6. Beckman, B., *#BlackLivesMatter saw tremendous growth on social media. Now what*? Retrieved from https://mashable.com/article/black-lives-matter-george-floyd-social-media-data/
7. As Corp Watch notes, Wellco Factory, in Dongguan, Chang'an is a Korean-invested factory contracted by Nike.

   > If they refuse they can be fined $1.20 – $3.61(10–30Rmb) or docked the entire day's pay. Several of the workers mentioned that they did not realise that they would be forced to work overtime when they were hired. The overtime of 2–4 hours (on top of the 11 hour work day) violates China's Labour Law, which allows for only 36 hours of overtime per month. The Labour Law and Nike's Code of Conduct both clearly state that coerced labour is not acceptable, yet workers in Wellco are forced to work long hours or they will be subject to termination.Company Watch (1997). *Working conditions in sports shoe factories in China, making shoes for Nike and Reebok*, September 1. Retrieved July 17, 2021, from www.corpwatch.org/article/working-conditions-sports-shoe-factories-china

8. Steller, T. (2018). *Chinese prison laborer's cry for help reaches Southern Arizona*, October 10. Retrieved July 13, 2021, from https://tucson.com/news/local/columnists/steller/steller-chinese-prison-laborer-s-cry-for-help-reaches-southern/article_21553c4b-404e-5ba7-8d73-7c9ceb8fbb17.html
9. Warren, R. (2018). You buy a purse at Walmart. There's a note inside from a "Chinese prisoner." Now what? *Vox*, October 10. Retrieved July 12, 2021, from www.vox.com/the-goods/2018/10/10/17953106/walmart-prison-note-china-factory
10. Trivedi, B. (2020). *Survey reveals geographic illiteracy*, November 20. Retrieved from www.nationalgeographic.com/science/article/geography-survey-illiteracy
11. Sherwood, H. (2020). Nearly two-thirds of US young adults unaware 6m Jews killed in the Holocaust. *The Guardian*, September 16. Retrieved July 13, 2021, from www.theguardian.com/world/2020/sep/16/holocaust-us-adults-study
12. Lankshear, C., & Knobel, M. (2008). *Digital literacies, concepts, policies and practices*. Peter Lang, p. 2.
13. ClientEarth. (2019). Lawyers take action against BP's climate "greenwashing advertising campaign". *Press Release*, December 4. Retrieved from www.clientearth.org/latest/press-office/press/lawyers-take-action-against-bp-s-climate-greenwashing-advertising-campaign/

7   The Dangers of a Single Story

Conventional Framing

Our curriculum often tells a single story from a white, western, male, high social economic status (SES) perspective. It is frequently told as the 'triumph' of western individuals over non-western and native cultures.

Reframing

Curriculum should recognize that there is not one story – but always multiple ones and it is the job of the educator to make students aware of the multiplicity of stories and views that always need to be incorporated into a more perfect account.

Guiding Questions

1. Why are we attracted to single story accounts and why should we resist their temptations?
2. What are some ways to avoid the binary trap?
3. How to apply a multi-perspective approach?

Schools are the places where the culture gets transmitted, but we are only just beginning to recognize that if it is just the dominant culture that is presented as the only one worth discussing students are not getting a fair understanding of the world they inhabit. Ever since the dawning of mass public education, school has just been about maintaining and distributing a storehouse of facts that serve the interests of the dominant culture; a story about American triumphs and very little about the world that suffered as a result of those so-called triumphs. We are improving all the time on that simplified view of the world but perhaps not as fast as we would like to think – the contributions of women, minorities and immigrants to the society are sometimes celebrated but too often they are sidelined and given second place to the largely white Anglo male actors who are afforded the status of 'founding fathers,' even as so many of them fought back the rights of others to be given basic rights to vote and participate in the democracy. It is easy to fall into the trap of seeing not just American history but the world through a lens of history winners. We have to keep reminding ourselves that history is written not by those whose lands were dispossessed, whose freedom and wealth was taken from them, but by the ones who succeeded in their task. But to view history as simply a choice between winners and losers versions of events is also a simplification. What a global perspective needs to take into account is that the interaction between a variety of global actors is important. The middlemen who made slavery possible – for example the West African traders who helped the Portuguese, Spanish and the English find the

DOI: 10.4324/9781003123903-10

Table 7.1 Contrasting traditional curriculum approaches with global ones

Traditional Curriculum Approaches	Global Curriculum Approaches
Single discipline	Multi-discipline
Single story	Multiple stories
Single perspective	Multiple perspectives
Relevance to students' lives limited	Relevance to students' lives expanded

slaves and export them; the ordinary citizens who smoked the tobacco and enjoyed the tea, coffee and sugar that brightened up their diets – all have stories to tell about the consequences of an institution like slavery. In other words it is not just a few people (usually white privileged males) who need to be at the center of our stories – we need to focus as well on the ordinary folk who built the ships to take the human and other cargos across the Atlantic and the people who financed them and consumed their goods.

What the global educator recognizes is that to understand these stories a global educator has to often cross disciplines, cross continents and make connections to the present day. Why? Because the tendency to see history and world events as removed from us and as purely an academic exercise limits our humanity. It is a recognition that we are all interconnected. Take for example a news story that appeared in the *Guardian* newspaper about the World Cup with the headline, "Revealed: 6,500 migrant workers have died in Qatar as it gears up for World Cup." With no worker regulations that protect migrants and the country committed to building seven new stadiums and dozens of major projects including a new airport, roads, public transport systems, hotels and even a new city, the result was to be foreseen.[1] Where does it belong in the global curriculum? It belongs in the long history of autocratic rulers who want to build their own monuments – we can go back to the Roman Colosseum or the building of the White House constructed from slave labor. The question is how we change our focus so that we begin to see the connections.

This chapter is about the value of multiple perspectives taking over the single story. As Table 7.1 shows moving away from the traditional curriculum opens up a new set of lenses to view other cultures free of any judgmental frames or set formats. The argument is clear – that we as teachers are not there to be storytellers and to provide society's narratives to the students that are both convenient and fit some larger paradigm; we are there to produce critical globally aware thinkers. To do this it is not just optional for students to see the other side of the case, whether they be oppressor or oppressed, white or black, native or invader. One argument against this is that the story gets confusing. Who are we going to believe? How do we extract from all of these voices either the facts or the stories that we can easily remember and regurgitate on a test? Yes this type of work is more complex – because it suggests that we are flying without a net. Most textbooks don't do multiple perspectives. We never learned how to do it when we were students so how do we turn our practice around?

Dangers of a Single Story

Chimamanda Adichie is a prize-winning Nigerian American author who grew up the daughter of a professor on a university campus but when she arrived in the US at the age of 19 she says that her American roommate was "shocked" – she wondered how Adichie had learned to speak English so well and wanted to know about her taste in "tribal music." The encounter raised a laugh when she related it in a highly popular TED talk but humor was not the point of the tale

74 *School and Classroom Approaches*

she had to tell – it was about the roommates' patronizing attitude to her as an African. As Adiche explains it,[2]

> My roommate had a single story about Africa. A single story of catastrophe. In this single story there was no possibility of Africans being similar to her, in any way. No possibility of feelings more complex than pity. No possibility of a connection as human equals. I must say that before I went to the U.S. I didn't consciously identify as African. But in the U.S. whenever Africa came up people turned to me. Never mind that I knew nothing about places like Namibia. But I did come to embrace this new identity. And in many ways I think of myself now as African.

Adiche does not vilify her room mate – but rather places herself in her shoes –

> If I had not grown up in Nigeria, and if all I knew about Africa were from popular images, I too would think that Africa was a place of beautiful landscapes, beautiful animals, and incomprehensible people, fighting senseless wars, dying of poverty and AIDS, unable to speak for themselves, and waiting to be saved, by a kind, white foreigner.

Adichie goes further – the attitude largely encouraged by colonialist white writers like Kipling is that it reinforces ignorance and is told by the powerful – the ones who have the power. As she writes,

> Power is the ability not just to tell the story of another person, but to make it the definitive story of that person. The Palestinian poet Mourid Barghouti writes that if you want to dispossess a people, the simplest way to do it is to tell their story, and to start with, "secondly." Start the story with the arrows of the Native Americans, and not with the arrival of the British, and you have an entirely different story. Start the story with the failure of the African state, and not with the colonial creation of the African state, and you have an entirely different story.

We should all as global educators see her magnificent TED Talk *in full* and have middle and high school students see it too. Not just because Adichie is an excellent communicator and can use humor to her advantage but because we all need to be reminded of the sadness of limiting people to one story – one stereotype limiting the possibility of connecting as human beings and as equals.

One of the most important ideas discussed by Adiche – is that stories have many starting points. The colonial story's starting point begins with the arrival of the invader – and treats those who are 'discovered' typically as not fully human. That is why the *New York Times' 1619 Project* is so important but incomplete – the approach taken by a team of *New York Times* writers led by Nikole Hannah-Jones is to argue that the true origin of the United States was not 1776 with the Declaration of Independence but with the arrivals of the first slaves from Portuguese-dominated Africa.[3] The narrative is compelling because it focuses on the fact that the creation of the US as a political entity is inextricably tied up with slavery. But as Wright points out, starting at 1619 involves another kind of erasure, "the names of American nations are signified only through an undifferentiated collective, 'indigenous people' and 'Native Americans.'" In other words, they too are reduced to a single story, one of crushing near-anonymity.[4] Through *1619*, the US becomes a nation born through slavery with only free whites and enslaved Black people populating it."[5]

What Are the Ways to Avoid the 'Binary Trap'?

A common objection to global education comes from the right who argue that schools should be focused on developing an American identity and that identity is incompatible with also owning

The Dangers of a Single Story 75

a global one. Crudely speaking, the right-wing view of the world is that America is not just an exceptional country (immune to some of the laws of history) but that nationality has some kind of racial basis so that it is not possible to conceive that you can be American and also share any kind of other national identity. The nationalists who make this argument have you in a binary trap. You can be either one thing or another – you cannot be both. The reality is that we can inhabit multiple identities. We can be both a Muslim, an American, a Dodgers fan, a daughter, a democrat. Our list of identities goes on and they don't have to cancel each one out. The beauty of being human, unlike a character in a novel or a picture on a wall, is that you can go from role to role and live within the frame of those identities for how long or little that you want. On July 4 you might feel more patriotic and in September as Ramadan begins more Muslim. There are no rules that control you or capacity to inhabit whatever identity you may feel as you yell for your home baseball team or worship along with your congregation. What is confusing is that others will want to ascribe an identity to you and want to narrow your options. Binary distinctions are favored by the powerful who wish to 'other' those who are deemed not to fit into the frame occupied by those with the power to define. By othering they want to make clear that the identity makes you into someone who is less than the human being they think they are. They want you to share their binary universe. A universe where fixed identities match up with beliefs and genetic histories – in other words they represent whether they are conscious of it or not a totalitarian regime where the party, church or autocrat decides who you really are and what value you represent. So the first lesson that counts is that you, not other people, get to define you. That is what makes Diogenes's famous remark when he was asked where he was from and said he was a citizen of the world. As the first cosmopolitan and cynic he founded an entire school of philosophers – the stoics further refined the idea to suggest that each human being as Hierocles states, "dwells . . . in two communities – the local community of our birth, and the community of human argument and aspiration." Hierocles began to develop the first effort to articulate the challenge that we all face as would-be "world citizens" to "draw the circles somehow towards the centre, making all human beings more like our fellow city dwellers." So almost right from the beginning the concept presented a radical challenge to those who regarded citizenship as synonymous with country and birthplace. It has not been an uncontroversial idea in the West where the right wing have tried to attack it from the view that it represents the encroachment of world government and some centralized control by a body like the United Nations that was heavily informed by the cosmopolitan ideas. But that political agenda is not in any way baked into cosmopolitanism, which only asks one to understand that there is one identity that unites us as citizens of the planet earth.

Disney – Turning Young People Into Consumers

This wide-ranging op ed by Henry Giroux and Grace Pollock, "How Disney Magic and the Corporate Media Shape Youth Identity in the Digital Age," discusses the ways that Disney was instrumental in shaping today's consumer culture that is increasingly being shared across the planet. The authors' analysis in particular of how they continue to promote that culture very early in the lives of children through such characters as the widely popular Hannah Montana is particularly disturbing. Here is an extract:

> The comment from *The New York Times* about Cyrus being a good role model for kids should be considered within this context of consumerism and what it teaches young girls in terms of their identities, values and aspirations. Hannah Montana is not a superhero, but merely a superstar whose only responsibility in life is to entertain her fans and make money. Miley Stewart's raison d'être is to deceive the people around her

76   *School and Classroom Approaches*

> so that she can live her life unencumbered by the social responsibilities attendant on being a well-known public figure. Finally, does not Cyrus, as the real-life embodiment of "three girls for the price of one," represent the most commodified of role models, severely and insidiously proscribing the imaginative possibilities for a generation of young women who are sadly being encouraged to view their bodies as objects, their identities as things to be bought and sold and their emotional and psychological health as best nurtured through "retail therapy" (shopping)?
>
> ### *Branding a Lifestyle*
>
> Have students review this video by Naomi Klein and a short blog that that summarizes key elements of her thesis:
> www.youtube.com/watch?v=lDTG_e7I4hU

How to Apply a Multi-Perspective Approach

Teachers often need new strategies to interrupt the single story narrative – curation which does not depend on single linear view of events can prove to be a useful tool to disrupt the way traditional narratives frame issues as heroic linear struggles. A curator moreover has the power to arrange just those people, images, objects or artifacts that strike them as significant and arrange them in meaningful ways.[6]

Today while not everyone can be in charge of an art collection they can now become authors of their own digital lives and many do through their interaction with Facebook and other social media. It is a short step for students to be given the opportunity to see the connections between different cultures, epochs, ethnicities and countries. There is no better way of exemplifying the idea of this form of curation than by reference to Neil McGregor's best-selling *A History of the World in 100 Objects*. Launched in 2010 as 15-minute radio broadcasts, the project morphed into a successful book, and an exhibition that has traveled the world's leading museums. One of the secrets to McGregor's success with this project is the foundational idea that objects have stories – and when you choose just 100 objects to tell the history of the world – those stories become more fascinating and less subject to easy one-story reductionism.

So for example one of the 100 objects he chooses to focus on is a jade axe, dated from some time between 4000 and 2000 bc, found near Canterbury, and made from jade. Through research it is discovered that the jade was quarried in the Italian Alps and the mystery is how it arrived in Canterbury some 600 miles away but the jade axe is significant because it was never used. It is one of the first examples of a utilitarian object that was treasured for its own artistic value. As McGregor concludes,

> That our axe has no signs of wear and tear is surely a consequence of the fact that its owners chose not to use it. This axe was designed to make a mark not on the landscape but in society, and its function was surely to be aesthetically pleasing. Its survival in such good condition suggests that people six thousand years ago found it just as beautiful as we do today. Our love of the expensive, the exquisite and the exotic, has a very long pedigree.[7]

Gratitude

Author A.J. Jacobs had the idea for a book based on a simple idea – how many people would he have to thank for his morning cup of coffee. You would suppose it would just be a handful – the barista who brewed his caffeine pick-me-up and those who shipped the beans and of course the growers. The number turns out to be close to 1,000 people to thank. The supply chain from the farmer who grew the beans in Columbia to the barista who served him was extensive. But this is also the reality of a global world – virtually every product we purchase has something produced in one or more countries and is involved in an extensive supply chain. Jacobs comes up with a beautiful metaphor taken from one of his favorite books *Invisible Cities* by Italo Calvino. The story features a fable of a city where people's apartments are connected by threads.

> Each thread represents a different kind of relationship. Eventually, the threads grow so numerous and thick and multi-shaded, it's impossible to walk through the city. If we connected the world with threads signifying gratitude, I realise, taking a sip of my coffee, the result would be as thick as a blanket.

Fear of the Other

Governments like people tend to other people or completely exclude them from history books. Case in point, as *New Yorker* writer Lauren Collins has pointed out, French students ignore the Haitian slave revolt. As Collins reports, most have never heard of Toussaint Louverture, who the scholar Sudhir Hazareesingh writes, was "the first black superhero of the modern age."[8] Although born enslaved on a sugar plantation on Saint-Domingue, a French colony on the island of Hispaniola, sometime in the early 1740s he led "the most important slave revolt in history, effectively forcing France to abolish slavery . . . outmaneuvered three successive French commissioners; defeated the British; overpowered the Spanish; and, in 1801 – despite having been wounded seventeen times in battle and having lost most of his front teeth to a cannonball explosion – authored a new abolitionist constitution for Saint-Domingue, asserting that "here, all men are born, live, and die free and French." Frederick Douglas hailed Louverture – as "the Black Spartacus," and although inspiring the modern anti-colonial movement France has more or less erased his name from the national narrative. On a much larger scale American textbooks have for decades elided the true horror of slavery and racism in the country. The global educator's challenge is not just to correct the erasures, the lies and the myth peddling but point to deeper truths – how all human societies have the tendency to reduce or even negate the contributions of minorities in the effort to render a seemingly coherent view of their national identity.

Schools have historically seen their role as socializing students into a relatively homogeneous national culture. It is a form of social conditioning that runs deep and is often hardly conscious. As Daniel Kahneman has argued in his widely praised book, *Thinking, Fast and Slow* – our brains have access to two decision-making processes, System 1 and System 2. System 1 allows us to process daily items quickly – such as automatically stopping at a red traffic light. System 2 is where we do more complex mental processing such as deciding whether or where we want to take a vacation. System 1 is the one that enables us to make snap judgments about people based on what they look or sound like.[9] It is a more primitive survival system. In the animal context that also applies to people it is known as 'fight or flight' when our body surges with adrenaline when confronted by a predator. What is clear is that System 1 is the place that often gets into trouble, because it is the place that harbors those implicit associations that lie outside of conscious awareness. What is important to note is that these implicit biases do not always align with any of our conscious beliefs. This means that as Stratt argues,

> even individuals who profess egalitarian intentions and try to treat all individuals fairly can still unknowingly act in ways that reflect their implicit – rather than their explicit – biases. Thus, even well-intentioned individuals can act in ways that produce inequitable outcomes for different groups.[10]

78 School and Classroom Approaches

Students should realize how powerful the System 1 responses are and can be factors in situations where people are under stress and have to make quick decisions – as we have seen with respect to multiple police killings of unarmed black men and women.

The question that global educators need to address is how to change implicit associations. One way as we note in Chapter 3 on pedagogy is to meaningfully engage with individuals whose identities (e.g. race, ethnicity, religion) differ from your own. Another approach is to expose students to counter-stereotypical examples: individuals who contradict widely held stereotypes. Finding films which feature female scientists – such as the movie *Hidden Figures* and men as carers or nurses, people from the Middle East who are problem solvers and community leaders might make some difference. Students might also try a mapping exercise that will help them identify the ways in which we use language to limit ourselves. Students might be given cards with names like uncle, aunt, as well as politicians and religious leaders and place them in certain quadrants of a frame like the one in Figure 7.1 – with the top quadrant referencing closeness of friendship and the bottom registering degrees of fear. Each person's map will be slightly different and the y axis related to the distance or frequency of contacts between you and the person. You must know the person – so when you refer to a store clerk or an immigrant – you can refer to him or her by their name or where they work.

The Power of Empathy

Another way to reduce othering – almost the brain's default pattern for many when someone new arrives into the community – is to encourage empathy. In one of Shakespeare's greatest unperformed speeches written in his own handwriting,[11] Sir Thomas More as embodied by Shakespeare

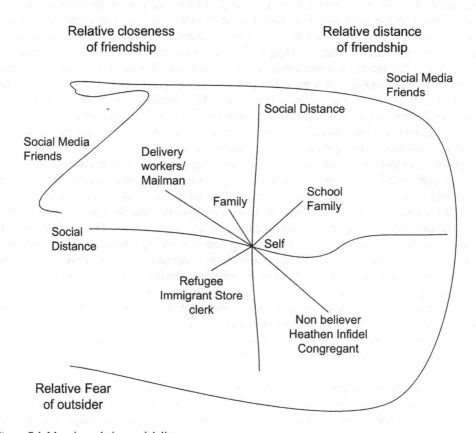

Figure 7.1 Mapping relative social distance

asks the rioters to imagine that they were in the refugees' shoes. Imagine that the king had granted their wish that the foreigners be "removed." Imagine them in other words as victims in a land where they will be considered strangers with rogues just like themselves whetting "their detested knives against your throats," as Shakespeare graphically describes their plight as on par with animals. The language is stark and Saxon; they would not be afforded "an abode on earth" and would be spurned "like dogs" as if they lost all their spiritual worth and dignity – "As if that God/Owed not nor made not you." Shakespeare ramps up his vivid imagery to break through the clouds of prejudice that transformed them into an angry heartless mob. Seeing the world from the eye of the stranger, the refugee, the outsider is a key shift as many educators have noted. Helping them to imagine the burden of being that person who they are used to scorning and belittling is just as much the work of the teacher as it is of the author.

The Book of Sir Thomas More, Act 2, Scene 4

Grant them removed, and grant that this your noise
Hath chid down all the majesty of England;
Imagine that you see the wretched strangers,
Their babies at their backs and their poor luggage,
Plodding to the ports and coasts for transportation,
And that you sit as kings in your desires,
Authority quite silent by your brawl,
And you in ruff of your opinions clothed;
What have you got? I'll tell you: you had taught
How insolence and strong hand should prevail,
How order should be quelled; and by this pattern
Not one of you should live an aged man,
For other ruffians, as their fancies wrought,
With self same hand, self reasons, and self right,
Would shark on you, and men like ravenous fishes
Would feed on one another. . . .
Say now the king
Should so much come too short of your great trespass
As to banish you, whither would you go?
What country, by the nature of your error,
Should give you harbour? go you to France or Flanders,
To any German province, to Spain or Portugal,
Nay, any where that not adheres to England,
Why, you must needs be strangers: would you be pleased
To find a nation of such barbarous temper,
That, breaking out in hideous violence,
Would not afford you an abode on earth,
Whet their detested knives against your throats,
Spurn you like dogs, and like as if that God
Owed not nor made not you, nor that the claimants
Were not all appropriate to your comforts,
But chartered unto them, what would you think
To be thus used? this is the strangers case;
And this your mountainish inhumanity.

School and Classroom Approaches

UN Ambassador Samantha Power spoke in a speech at the Lincoln Center Global Exchange in 2015 that

> Thomas More's speech to the mob is as relevant as ever. . . . The 'wretched strangers' have changed of course, from the Lombards targeted in 1517 in those riots to the Huguenot refugees in Shakespeare's time and to the Syrians, Iraqis, South Sudanese, Eritreans and others fleeing repressive governments of our time.[12]

A global teacher might usefully follow Shakespeare's two steps towards empathy with the stranger – first the act to imagine their plight as if they were observers or journalists reporting on the human rights violation and then secondly placing themselves in the actual shoes of the person who has been victimized. Clearly there are some useful ways to do this for any historical period – from the experience of Jews in Egypt being forced to be slaves, to the refugees and migrants who are desperately trying to leave war zones in the Middle East (see Appendix).

The simple fact is that we are preparing our students to live in a global community. They will be traveling, texting and videoconferencing with a wider variety of people from across the globe than ever before. A single story, a single viewpoint or a simple narrative will not allow us to reach the levels of understanding, empathy and cross-cultural communication we need to thrive in this new world. As Adiche has stated,

> I've always felt that it is impossible to engage properly with a place or a person without engaging with all of the stories of that place and that person. The consequence of the single story is this: It robs people of dignity. It makes our recognition of our equal humanity difficult. It emphasizes how we are different rather than how we are similar.[13]

Notes

1. Pattison, P. (2021). Revealed: 6,500 migrant workers have died in Qatar since World Cup awarded. *The Guardian*, February 23. Retrieved July 14, 2021, from www.theguardian.com/global-development/2021/feb/23/revealed-migrant-worker-deaths-qatar-fifa-world-cup-2022
2. Adichie, C. (2009, July). *TED Talk.* Retrieved July 14, 2021, from kwww.ted.com/talks/chimamanda_ngozi_adichie_the_danger_of_a_single_story/transcript
3. The 1619 (2019, August 14). The 1619 Project. *The New York Times*, August 17, 2019. Retrieved July 14, 2021, www.nytimes.com/interactive/2019/08/14/magazine/1619-america-slavery.html
4. Wright, M. (2020). 1619: The danger of a single origin story. *American Literary History*, *32*(4), e1–e12, https://doi.org/10.1093/alh/ajaa027. Retrieved from https://academic.oup.com/alh/article/32/4/e1/5903561
5. Many commentators have pushed back on the narrative that 1619 was the beginning of the American nation. Dawn Custalow for example writing in the *Virginian Pilot* argues that to "propose that 1619 was the beginning of this nation denies the recognition of the Powhatans and their present-day descendants who continue to live on and outside of the Mattaponi and Pamunkey Indian reservations today. How can any group of people reframe another's history "See Native Americans still overlooked in debates about U.S. history, *Virginian Pilot*. Retrieved September 26, 2020, from https://www.pilotonline.com/opinion/columns/vp-ed-column-custalow-0927-20200926-aof7b2j4brgbzmwbess7ywhirm-story.html
6. Curation is an odd word dating back to the Roman Empire when Curatores, as they were called, were paid government employees with the directive to build out the infrastructure of the Empire, including the great roads and aqueducts that served as the empire's infrastructure. In 14th-century France, the word morphed into a different kind of organizer – a Curé was a priest who could take 'care of souls' through his ability to create spiritual meaning for his parishioners. It was only in the 20th century that this complex word was applied to the people in a museum that provided order and context to art collections.
7. BBC, *A history of the world in 100 objects*. Retrieved from www.bbc.co.uk/programmes/articles/4CBt tcJSM6N1hZKpHs67b1z/episode-transcript-episode-14-jade-axeb
8. Collins, L. (2020). The Haitian Revolution and the hole in French high-school history. *New Yorker*, December 3. Retrieved July 17, 2021, from www.newyorker.com/culture/culture-desk/the-haitian-revolution-and-the-hole-in-french-high-school-history

The Dangers of a Single Story   81

9. Kahneman, D. (2012). Of 2 minds: How fast and slow thinking shape perception and choice [Excerpt]. *Scientific American*, June 15. Retrieved July 14, 2021, from www.scientificamerican.com/article/kahneman-excerpt-thinking-fast-and-slow/

10. Staats, C. (2015–2016). Understanding implicit bias: What educators should know. *American Educator*, *29*, 30. Retrieved July 14, 2021, from https://files.eric.ed.gov/fulltext/EJ1086492.pdf

11. The Book of Sir Thomas More: Shakespeare's only surviving literary manuscript. *British Library*. Retrieved July 17, 2021, from www.bl.uk/collection-items/shakespeares-handwriting-in-the-book-of-sir-thomas-more#

12. Quartz, A. (2016). The banned 400-year-old Shakespearean speech being used for refugee rights today. *Huffington Post*, September 21.

13. Adichie, C., *The danger of a single story: Transcript courtesy of TED*. Retrieved from www.hohschools.org/cms/lib/NY01913703/Centricity/Domain/817/English%2012%20Summer%20Reading%20-%20 2018.pdf

8 Maximizing the 'Global' in Global Education Technology

Conventional Framing

Education technology is used in limited ways in schools, for research, presentations, etc. as well as games but has so far failed to transform learning and teaching or significantly extend global understanding.

Reframing

Because the Internet allows every classroom on the planet to be connected, today's teacher is presented with a unique opportunity to turn their classroom into a more active force as a critical tool for understanding the world guided by curiosity and interpersonal connection.

Guiding Questions

1. Why do changes in global media technology require a new approach to teaching?
2. What are some key social media issues teachers should focus on?
3. How can we maximize the value of global learning platforms?

Imagine the typical family of the 1960s surrounding the TV set sitting there (perhaps with a TV dinner resting on a coffee table) taking in the national newscasts and being largely silent as they bathe in the rays emanating from the cathode ray screen. Contrast that scene with the modern family of 2021 with everyone in the family using a different device and accessing a different social media platform, with dad or mom also on a Zoom call for work or with a distant family relative. What has occurred? It is not easy to characterize but essentially it is all about the plethora of consumer choices, the shriveling up of what might be termed community space and consensus.

What is less easy to discern is that this modern family now could be situated more or less anywhere on the globe where a consumer society may be said to exist. According to industry sources the number of smartphone users in the world today is 3.8 billion, or 48.46% of the world's population. In total, the number of people that own a smart and feature phone is 4.88 billion, making up 62.24% of the world's population (Figure 8.1).[1] Although there is significant penetration as Figure of these devices in the west there are still as Figure 7.1 shows some basic divides between the global north and south. Going deeper -the Covid19 Pandemic revealed, "nearly half of all parents with lower incomes stated it would have to do their schoolwork just using a cell phone.[2]

The old way of relating to a world where information was mediated by three national TV companies or even one broadcaster such as Walter Cronkite has gone for good; we are in the multichannel, multi-platform universe and we should try to make the best use of it that we can. This chapter will argue that there are many sound ways to have students investigate their interests

DOI: 10.4324/9781003123903-11

Maximizing 'Global' in Global Education 83

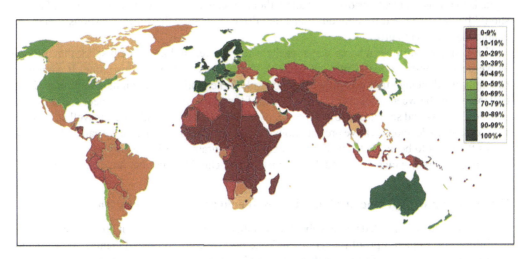

Figure 8.1 Mobile phone use as a percentage of population
Source: https://upload.wikimedia.org/wikipedia/commons/b/bc/Mobile_phone_use_world2.PNG

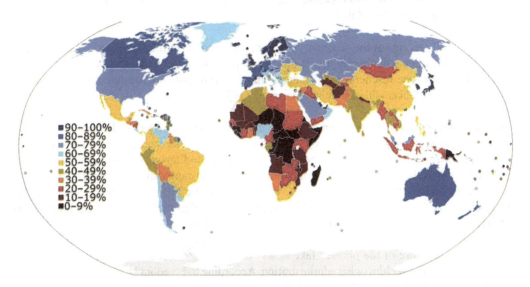

Figure 8.2 Internet users in 2015 as a percentage of a country's population
Source: International Telecommunications Union

about the world, confront their prejudices, construct presentations that help them transcend their typical ability to articulate their response to the world and allow their voices to make a real difference. These modalities are different from the opportunities available in the standard classroom of a decade or more ago and if truth be admitted most classrooms today. They ask the teacher to share some of the excitement of having a channel into the world that can help transcend school's usual boundaries.

Our gadgets all depend on the user's attention span – all of us have been trained to gain what is often called a dopamine rush when we interact with an image that we enjoy. We as educators have a hard time adjusting to this reality – we like to nurture a longer attention span but viewed in a different way we can use this attention span issue to our advantage. The way forward I shall

84 *School and Classroom Approaches*

argue is to release student curiosity and allow them to roam as they seek to find meaning. Passion should be the driver and it is the questions that drive students – their own questions – that will enable that passion to grow.

This chapter will look at some ways teachers can use technology to help spark that passion as we develop more globally minded citizens. Technology cannot do this alone. It cannot be re-emphasized enough that it is only a tool to explore the world – through its ability to assist in collaborations between students in remote areas of the globe, its ability to connect students with decision makers and so help establish the students' sense of agency and voice as well as to motivate students to develop creative presentations for real audiences. But before we can address these topics there has to be an understanding of the media-saturated world we now inhabit – students need media literacy which has all but been wiped out in school by the Common Core curriculum.[3]

What Are Some Key Social Media Issues Teachers Should Focus On?

Students should be reminded that Facebook is a global company and while it does not want to use the billions of dollars in profit (generated in large part by consumers like themselves who may not understand that the information they generate by clicking on various buttons is the product that Facebook sells to its advertisers) to educate its consumers, it now has to police a realm where anything-goes speech has caused untold deaths and destruction of communities. A recent report by the Pew Foundation found that

> "nearly 80 percent (of the secondary teachers surveyed) described (their students') 'limited ability to evaluate the credibility of online information' as a moderate or major problem." 92 percent of the teachers said "students must learn to critically evaluate information for credibility and bias – it's a crucial citizenship skill."

Stanford University researchers found that the inability of even college students to discern fact from fiction was a "threat to democracy."[4] When it comes to social media we now know the way conspiracy theories have found their home on the Internet and thrive, helped in many cases by governments who have highly trained individuals who can instantly spread disinformation about the world to advance their nation's interests. While there is renewed interest among some legislators both in the federal government and in the states to develop media literacy approaches it is clearly up to individual teachers to do their part in helping students through the thicket of misinformation. Any major media company is now of necessity a global one. Take former President Trump's repeated use of the phrase "fake news" to more or less describe any information that seemed hostile to either him or his administration. According to Freedom House, between January 2017 and May 2019, at least 26 countries "enacted or introduced laws or regulations providing for censorship or criminal prosecution of 'fake news.'"[5] Those governments include repressive regimes like Egypt, Poland, Hungary, Turkey, South Korea and the Philippines. Florida recently passed a law that essentially criminalizes an accepted democratic right to protest. Other states are also considering similar measures that will subject the right to protest to criminal penalties if the authorities judge that their activity will lead to rioting. "The American Civil Liberties Union views the law as a dangerous infringement on civil liberties since it gives police broad discretion over what constitutes a demonstration and a riot."[6] Demagogues increasingly use social media to their advantage – constantly pumping out inflammatory footage that is designed not to win arguments using logic and reason but through their opposite, provoking emotional reactions designed to block rational thought. With regard to the recent Covid19 pandemic the World Health Organization as well as other health authorities have become increasingly alarmed at what they call an "infodemic," a combination of misinformation that is generated by WhatsApp groups and social media platforms that draw upon hoaxes and conspiracy theories surrounding Covid19.[7]

Maximizing 'Global' in Global Education   85

In this very unstable environment we must help provide our students some of the tools that they need to resist the war that in particular anti-democratic demagogues are waging against truth to serve their own goals and purposes. There are a few ways to help your students identify fake news but they have to practice them constantly.

Adapted from FactCheck

1. What is the source of the news? Is it a reputable news source – one that has a history of reliable reporting such as the *New York Times* or the BBC? If you cannot decide, take a look at the ratio of ads to content. If the ads are as prominent as the content, you may get suspicious. Check the web address: it may be suspicious if it is not a straight proper noun followed by a dot com.
2. Is it opinion or factually based? One way to tell if it is factual is that sources are referenced. What kind of sources are used – eyewitnesses, reputable experts and organizations?
3. Is this story being covered by other news outlets? If it is, there is some degree of confidence that the event took place.
4. Read beyond the headline – a common lazy habit that we all get into from time to time is not to read past the headline. Fake news writers know this and will deliberately set out headlines that provoke visceral reactions. *Read beyond the headline.* As the Annenberg Institute writes,

    > Even in legitimate news stories, the headline doesn't always tell the whole story. But fake news, particularly efforts to be satirical, can include several revealing signs in the text. That abcnews.com.co story that *we checked*, headlined "Obama Signs Executive Order Banning the Pledge of Allegiance in Schools Nationwide," went on to quote "Fappy the Anti-Masturbation Dolphin." We have to assume that the many readers who asked us whether this viral rumor was true hadn't read the full story.

5. Check who wrote the article – most responsible news sources will include the name of the writer and a hyperlink to their name and often bio.

Why is this important? Hannah Arendt said it best when she spoke about how the "ideal subject of totalitarian rule" is not "the convinced Nazi or the convinced Communist, but people for whom the distinction between fact and fiction (ie the reality of experience) and the distinction between true and false (ie the standards of thought) no longer exist."

Media Literacy Resources

"Teaching resources already exist. *News Literacy Project*, for example, has a free 13-lesson *online curriculum*. Its lessons also cover topics like 'deep fake' videos and the role of journalism in a democracy.

Other resources include *Ground News*, which compares reportage; *Adfontes Media*, which assesses the reliability of news sources; and *Media Education Foundation*, which makes documentaries about media's impact."

86 *School and Classroom Approaches*

One way a globally minded teacher might think about the issue is through the lens of a company like Facebook that has nearly a quarter of the world's population (over two billion users) consuming its services.

In other words we have left a fairly stable media environment of the 1990s to a more chaotic one that separates out according to age and social class.

Students Must Learn About the Destabilizing Potential of Social Media

Hate speech enabled by Facebook led the Sri Lankan government in March 2020 to be shut down at the height of the violence. "This whole country could have been burning in hours," a government spokesperson reportedly told the *Guardian*.[8] As a result of mounting pressure to do something or governments would step in and regulate, Facebook's CEO Mark Zuckerberg founded a supreme court to adjudicate what types of speech and what individuals would be banned from using the platform. The challenge could not be more daunting, as Facebook morphs from being less like a corporation and more like an unelected world government. Facebook has in some ways created a teachable moment for us all as it works to establish a supreme court to adjudicate who should be given a platform and who should be denied one.

Students need to engage in the censorship issues that arise from social media's status as a global media enterprise. Questions such as can a universal standard be constructed need to be debated. By way of some background, in 2020 Facebook created forums in Singapore, New Delhi, Nairobi, Mexico City, Berlin, and New York. To see if the company could find some consensus around capitals such as Nairobi, that might at least guide the court to come up with a rule that could be globally enforced on the network. They reportedly began the discussion with a test photo that featured a photo of a smiling girl with a comic book caption that stated "Kill All Men," to determine whether consensus was possible. People in the forums were split between banning this violent speech while others believed that it should not be banned as the image was satirically designed to point to the way that those whose voices have been suppressed are typically not considered a threat, but generating humor in this way is not a luxury that many countries that have known large-scale political violence can afford. Helping students to understand these kinds of cultural nuances can be the beginning of students' global technology awareness.

What Facebook found was a mixed bag of results – as Kate Klonick reported for *The New Yorker*, "In New York, for example, sixty per cent of people voted to reinstate the 'Kill All Men' post, but only forty per cent did so in Nairobi." While a majority of New Yorkers saw no harm in the image, those who had lived under authoritarian regimes saw the photograph differently.[9] Regional governments in Ethiopia have been responsible for stoking ethnic violence via Facebook. The situation has become so dire that UN human rights chief Michelle Bachelet warned the situation in Ethiopia could "spiral totally out of control, leading to heavy casualties and destruction" and said "fighting must stop immediately to prevent further atrocities." As the BBC reported, even Ethiopian running legend Haile Gebrselassie has told the BBC that fake news shared on Facebook was behind violence in which 78 people died.[10]

But students need also to understand that Facebook has organized itself to heighten controversy because controversy equals increased engagement, and increased engagement translates into increased revenue. Zephyr Teachout, a law professor at Fordham argues that if we want less inflammatory speech, Facebook would have to make a business decision to drop targeted advertising, which incentivizes the promotion of incendiary, attention-grabbing posts. "If the core of our communications infrastructure is driven by targeted ads, we will have a toxic, conflict-driven communications sphere," she said. The dropping of targeted ads will never happen, and she also argues that the company is too big and needs to be broken up through antitrust litigation.

Not everyone is ready for this in-depth analysis but it is clear that if you are going to teach global educational technology there are some easy ways to do so, such as viewing the excellent

Social Dilemma that was produced in 2020 and directed by Jeff Orlowski and written by Orlowski, Davis Coombe and Vickie Curtis. The movie shows through a docudrama format how the business model is based on assisting users to follow their interests that eventually turn into addictions as the brain rewards the addict with additional pleasurable doses of dopamine. The docudrama links these trends to a rise in teenage suicide and increased political polarization.

What Are the Most Effective Ways to Use Technology to Assist Global Learning?

Célestin Freinet: A Founding Father of Global Education Technology

At the close of the First World War a wounded Frenchman, Célestin Freinet, returned home from the war. He was suffering from a lung injury when, lacking a college degree, he applied for a teaching job at the local village elementary school. He had one issue – the lung injury he had sustained strained his voice so he needed to find ways to control as well as engage using minimal vocal effort. The result was not a disaster – but led towards the creation of a very different child-centered classroom. His brilliant insight was to find a primitive printing press he could use to produce both a school newspaper, *Le Journal Scolaire* (*School Journal*), and a class journal, *Livre de Vie* (*Book of Life*). This idea would have been advanced for the 1920s but not revolutionary – the next idea occurred when fellow teacher Rene Daniel was reading Freinet's articles in *Clarity* and the *Emancipated School*, and recognizing a fellow free spirit, started a correspondence followed with him. The two exchanged small essays, poems written by their students and grouped into 'books of life.' This exchange then included parcels of interesting artifacts from each of the villages and then short films shot in 9.5 mm Pathé. Word of this exchange spread and so a network of school connections formed until 1933 when Hitler's rise put an end to this kind of educational experimentation.

The work of Freinet and Daniel was later expanded with the creation of clusters, consisting of several school partnerships all matched for age and curriculum interest, that included sending sample projects back and forth using the postal service as the means of communication. These exchanges included collaborative writing using the printing press that had been the foundation of Freinet's classroom approach. The partnerships were formalized in 1928 as the Public Educators' Co-operative (La Coopérative de L'Enseignement Laïc, CEL), and included other emerging technologies such as movies and tape recordings. From these beginnings grew a network that extended to 10,000 schools around the world. As a tribute to Freinet's influence, teachers in France today can send parcels free of charge as long as they serve an educational purpose. Followers such as the Italian educator Mario Lodi translated Freinet's message to Italian schools when he formed the Cooperative Education Movement in 1951 with schools around the world. This chapter in the history of educational technology is frequently ignored or minimized. We tend to think that it is all about the invention of the first personal computers and then the development of the Internet that transformed their potential from limited devices to, among other things, windows on the world.

The Internet provides teachers today with an unprecedented amount of opportunities to engage students in interpersonal learning. It cannot be stressed enough how important exposure to another viewpoint is for students' ability to reduce their prejudices about others who look and sound different from themselves. There is a vast amount of literature on that key aspect of student

88   *School and Classroom Approaches*

growth – a literature that owes a vast amount to the grandfather of child psychology Jean Piaget, who was one of the first people to understand the cognitive change that occurs in children when they first interact with another child. In the concrete operational stage (7–11) children begin to understand that the world does not circle around them and begin to understand that others have a different perspective.[11]

As Boix Mansilla and Jackson (2011) state,

> the ability to recognize the perspectives of others is not an optional skill for students to learn in the 21st century because they will encounter those of differing beliefs in multicultural work environments, academic studies, or personal relationships. Simply using technology as a device cannot magically conjure up the rich learning that can often occur when people from different cultures connect.

So as the OECD reminds us,

> a supply-driven and hardware-focused approach to technology does not help, and may even be counterproductive. The mere presence of technology is not by itself enough for innovation. Going digital may only reproduce traditional methods and pedagogies in a different form.[12]

But before all that can begin there needs to be some preliminary steps taken so that students display the most productive attitudes and dispositions to online learning.

How Can We Maximize the Value of Global Learning Platforms?

For at least a century the art of students connecting with other students has been the privilege of very fortunate students who attended mostly private schools where pen pals were seen as a safe kind of hobby for those who intended to have lives involving travel.

I remember signing up for one such service and looking forward to the sometimes bulky airmail letters that arrived informing me of 'friends' in France and Germany hobbies and sports exploits. All very harmless fun but a step in the process of realizing that there were other children who shared similar and relatively boring adolescent lives. Still there was something special about the pen friend – something that allowed you to have a private window into another world. Martyn Barrett, a leading researcher in this area, regards intercultural learning as critical and cites an impressive amount of research to suggest that intergroup contact can reduce prejudice toward people from other cultural groups, but provides four conditions that need to operate to maximize that affect. Both groups need to[13]

1. Perceive themselves to be of equal status within the contact situation.
2. Be sufficiently prolonged and close that it has the potential to allow meaningful relationships or friendships to develop between the participants.
3. Involve cooperation on joint activities that are aimed at achieving common goals (rather than competition between groups).
4. Be backed by an explicit framework of support by those in authority or by social institutions.

Barrett concludes that "these conditions mean that, in the school context, simply bringing students from different cultural backgrounds into contact with one another may not be sufficient for reducing prejudice. Instead, students who have different cultural affiliations need to cooperate within the classroom on tasks where they have common goals. Without the benefit of the Internet and a number of websites dedicated to intercultural connection (listed under Other Resources) this challenge may be near impossible to manage. There are now platforms that are designed to cater to every need. For a teacher who wants just to test the waters so to speak and wants a one-time contact for a project she is working on, there is Empatico, for example, a free tool for educators focused on the ages 6–11 – "because children at this age are old enough to understand their role in the world, but young enough to be positively influenced by experiences." As the Covid19 epidemic has increasingly made schooling a riskier option for many parents – Empatico is an ideal gift for homeschoolers – it instantly reduces isolation and offers the fortunate the chance for a cross-cultural friendship. For the classroom teacher who likes project-based work, ePals has stood the test of time as a staple for many. Founded in 1996, ePals and the ePals Global Learning Community includes some 4.5 million students and teachers in 200 countries, making it the largest online communities in K-12 education. As well as offering teacher-to-teacher and teacher-to-student communications, pen pal exchanges, you can easily connect on the Collaborative Projects link to find several ready-to-use projects (Self Driving Cars, Hamilton, Habitats, Maps, Natural Disasters, Water, and others). The range of projects is very impressive – for example, the site even contains what they term "Global volunteer opportunities," which start with writing and exchanging volunteer profiles with a group of students in a partnering classroom with similar interests. Both sets of students then use the partner group's profile to research volunteer opportunities in their community.

The most popular of the ePals menu is the project page where classroom teachers advertise their interests and invite other teachers to connect.

ePals, now run by McGraw Hill, is one of the great success stories of e-learning and cultural connection and is often overlooked as a resource for its special value for elementary and middle school students in particular who may be located in remote and more rural areas of the country with minimal international contact. The great advantage of these learning platforms is the way they offer a degree of choice and control of how they want to approach global awareness. A teacher beginning this process would clearly have to know their students' interests and their objectives and can begin a productive dialogue with them as they are offered choices as to which countries and which classrooms within those countries they want to work with.[14]

Conclusion

Collaboration of any kind let alone involving international connections that require juggling of time zones and classroom logistics, not to mention language are highly demanding. All this takes time and resources that most teachers don't have. It is depressing but true that most of the schools that have fully taken the global education mandate on board are wealthy independent schools that dot the world's capitals and absorb well-paid international workers who appreciate a highly rigorous well-respected international baccaularatte (IB) curriculum. That aside, one of the significantly weak areas is professional development. Most teachers do not realize the plethora of resources that exist to assist in any global project. But to do so, as we have discussed, they have to do a lot of time-consuming work, including

1. Identifying an actionable issue.

   The issue should be related to a goal that the students care about. It is not about what you care about – it is about what they care about.

2. Connecting with a relevant curriculum standard.
3. Preparing!

   In order for a collaboration to be successful, it is important that students learn some more about the culture they are about to encounter. To further minimize risks of misunderstandings,

90   *School and Classroom Approaches*

students might learn at least some key words in the other's language, and how you show respect in that culture.

4. Developing an assessment strategy as many of these projects extend over several weeks.

One of the key goals is to help the learner see the issues from the viewpoint of the other person/culture – so assessment might be more important than a checklist (where you identify easily measurable metrics such as how long the conversation, the numbers of times that the student used a word in the other's language, etc. – all important) – but also include pre- and post-answers to questions about the topic to see how those early views were changed as a result of the conversation.

5. Needing to build trust if they want this to be more than just an exercise.

In order to promote a sense of community, students should be allowed to email and connect offline through social media platforms such as Instagram.

To move forward you need both the well-founded belief that these kinds of cultural exchanges can move students from a routine type of global awareness to a more fully formed engagement. There can be no substitute for the joy that can come from working with someone who has a completely different perspective on an issue. As Ariel Tichnor-Wagner states,

at its core, global learning is about facilitating educational experiences that allow students to appreciate diverse perspectives, understand the connections they have to the wider world, respectively and effectively communicate and collaborate across cultures and countries, and use disciplinary and interdisciplinary knowledge to investigate and take action on issues that matter to them and the wider world.[15]

Notes

1. BankmyCell, *Number of mobile phone & smartphone users*. Retrieved July 17, 2021, from www.bankmycell.com/blog/how-many-phones-are-in-the-world
2. Lake, R., & Makori, The Digital Divide Among Students During COVID-19: Who Has Access? Who Doesn't? *CPRE Reinventing Public Education*. Retrieved from https://www.crpe.org/thelens/digital-divide-among-students-during-covid-19-who-has-access-who-doesnt
3. Baker, F., Short and sweet: Here's what Frank Baker is going to tell policymakers this year. *Media Literacy Now*. Retrieved from https://medialiteracynow.org/making-the-case-for-media-literacy/
4. *Students have 'dismaying' inability to tell fake news from real, study finds*. Retrieved from www.npr.org/sections/thetwo-way/2016/11/23/503129818/study-finds-students-have-dismaying-inability-to-tell-fake-news-from-real
5. Editorial Board. (2020). Trump's contempt for truth leaves a toxic legacy around the world. *Washington Post*, September 23, p.A22. Retrieved July 17, 2012, from www.washingtonpost.com/opinions/2020/09/22/trump-contempt-truth-editorial/
6. Florida signs 'anti-rioting, pro-law enforcement' bill into law, *CBS News*, April 20, 2021. Retrieved July17, 2021, from https://wtop.com/national/2021/04/florida-signs-anti-rioting-pro-law-enforcement-bill-into-law/
7. *1st WHO infodemiology conference*. Retrieved July 17, 2021, from www.who.int/news-room/events/detail/2020/06/30/default-calendar/1st-who-infodemiology-conference
8. Hogan, L., & Safi, M. (2018). Revealed: Facebook hate speech exploded in Myanmar during Rohingya crisis. *The Guardian*, April 2. Retrieved July 18, 2021, from www.theguardian.com/world/2018/apr/03/revealed-facebook-hate-speech-exploded-in-myanmar-during-rohingya-crisis
9. Klonick, K. (2012). Inside the making of Facebook's Supreme Court. *New Yorker*, February 12. Retrieved July 18, 2021, from www.newyorker.com/tech/annals-of-technology/inside-the-making-of-facebooks-supreme-court
10. BBC. (2019). *Ethiopia violence: Facebook to blame, says runner Gebrselassie*, November 2. Retrieved July 18, 2021, from www.bbc.com/news/world-africa-50276603
11. Guarino, G. (2020). Jean Piaget's theory of cognitive development. *Psych Point*, July 10. Retrieved July 18, 2021, from www.psychpoint.com/mental-health/articles/jean-piagets-theory-of-cognitive-development/

12. *OECD educational research and innovation, schools at the crossroads of innovation in cities and regions*. Retrieved July 18, 2021, from www.oecd-ilibrary.org/sites/9789264282766-en/1/1/2/index. html?itemId=/content/publication/9789264282766-en&_csp_=63d6472e57530b73be8d80e2f105d9f1 &itemIGO=oecd&itemContentType=book#execsumm-1
13. Barrett, M., How schools can promote the intercultural competence of young people. *European Psychologist*, *23*(1), 93–104. Retrieved July 18, 2021, from www.researchgate.net/publication/323852080_ How_Schools_Can_Promote_the_Intercultural_Competence_of_Young_People/link/5fc52a7f92851c 3012974ff5/download.
14. As Tiven and Fuchs's report points out,

> students ages 10 to 13 increasingly define their interests and demonstrate areas of increased awareness by selecting topics that they view as relevant to themselves. At earlier learning levels, students passively identify areas of interest, but as they individualize and develop a sense of self-efficacy, they tend to revisit and redefine their interests based on activities in which they are or could be involved. These processes signal potential for global engagement because, taken together, they constitute the learners' receptiveness to global subject matter and the sense that they have an active part to play.

> Nicaise, G., & Crane (2000). Indicators include interest in global issues (43-GE) and recognition of one's capacity to advocate for and contribute to local, regional, or global improvement (45-GE).

15. Tichnor-Wagner, A. (2018). Why global education matters. *ASCD*, March 8, 2018. Retrieved July 18, 2021, from www.ascd.org/blogs/why-global-education-matters

9 Global Education and School Culture

Conventional Framing

While there is general support for students to become more globally aware on the part of business leaders as well as politicians, there are many competing priorities for schools to focus on that are more deserving of attention.

Reframing

Schools must take global awareness from an optional choice made by a few teachers to a mission owned by the entire school.

Guiding Questions

1. Why are school-wide approaches so critical?
2. Why do we need to begin with a school mission statement?
3. Why is it important to overcome schools' resistance to embracing global competency?
4. What other initiatives can principals take to promote global competencies?

Why Are School-Wide Approaches so Critical?

Individual teachers cannot develop more globally aware students alone – they need the help of the entire school to help shift their naturally nationalistic perspective. It is inevitable that over 200 years of tax-supported public schools means that schools feel themselves an arm of the state and duty bound to support a nationalistic perspective. But schools also have a responsibility to develop student's critical intelligence and they need to resist promoting a simple patriotic agenda. During times of war the temptations to follow the party line can be overwhelming but in this period where most countries are committed to what might be considered a 'globalization agenda,' schools must try to try to strike a more balanced approach. The reality is that schools have tremendous power over young people – not just over the formal curriculum with the choices of textbooks, exams and syllabuses – but also the informal one. As Roland Barth, author of *Improving Schools from Within*, argues, it is the attitudes and dispositions that the adults show with respect to their relationships with both students and with each other that determine how much of the learning really sticks. It is the "nature of relationships among the adults within a school that has a greater influence on the character and quality of that school and on student accomplishment than anything else."[1] The most recent PISA analysis concerning global competencies confirms the fact that schools' importance in helping develop global

DOI: 10.4324/9781003123903-12

competencies cannot be underestimated: "schools can provide a safe space in which students can explore complex and controversial global issues that they encounter through the media and their own experiences."[2] In this regard, the role of school leaders, particularly in this new more diverse environment is pivotal. They have a responsibility to create a school climate conducive to tolerance and understanding of difference. We need to be reminded again and again that attitudes of respect to those from other backgrounds are not automatic – they need to be learned from behavior that is modeled by adults.

The most recent Programme for International Student Assessment (PISA) results, titled "Are Students Ready to Thrive in an Interconnected World?", clearly indicates that education systems that are most successful in preparing young people to thrive in interconnected circumstances feature whole-school approaches that:

1. Support positive learning environments with curricula that value openness to the world.
2. Offer opportunities to relate to people from other cultures, including through international exchanges and virtual programs.
3. Provide participatory learning activities based on real-world happenings.
4. Feature teachers who are prepared to foster global competence and inclusion.

The report argues that global competence can be more effectively fostered by a school-wide approach that includes education stakeholders including parents, community groups and organizations, and other programs that expose students to other cultures.

MacFarland et al., after combing through many studies, found that what makes a difference to global understanding are some small things, for example:[3]

- Celebration of global events such as UN day as a school unit
- Opportunities for service learning and study abroad
- Invitation of guest speakers who can highlight the connection between local and global
- Encouragement of the study of foreign languages
- Sponsorship of extracurricular activities that promote global learning, such as visits to international cultural events like a touring arts group

Reysen and Katzarska-Miller (2013c) found that the school environment could be enhanced by adding global citizenship terminology to school mission and vision statements, highlighting classes that contain global components and generally highlighting connections between the school and the world.

What became clear from the analyses of PISA 2018 data is that those countries where students reported that they engaged in more than five activities apart from direct learning and instruction at school, including discussion, participation in cultural events and following the news on the Internet or by reading newspapers, did better on global competency assessments.[4]

> Students' reports were confirmed by those of their school principals. According to school principals, the most common learning activities were learning about the beliefs, norms, values, customs and arts of diverse cultural groups and learning about different cultural perspectives on historical and social events. The least common activities were celebrations of festivities of other cultures and student exchanges with schools from other countries.

Clearly what the school does in terms of using students' informal learning makes a critical difference. The Asia Society provides plenty of examples of the way these activities or student-led clubs and societies can engage in global issues.

94　*School and Classroom Approaches*

International School Newspaper

Each year since fall 2005, 15 students have come together to produce International Insider, the high school newspaper of the College of Staten Island High School for International Studies (CSI) in New York City. They tackle tough topics in every issue. From global warming and genocide in Darfur to war in Iraq and Lebanon, it's a tricky charge, but these students are game. CSI students are in constant dialogue with student reporters in Bahrain, Belarus, Egypt, Poland, Ramallah, Saudi Arabia and Syria. Before each issue, students discuss ideas for articles via email and settle on a special topic. "Working on the paper is a chance to explore the world one teenager at a time," offered Anam Baig, one of the student senior editors from CSI. "The articles we receive from teens from around the world are pure, uncensored accounts." Students edit for factual accuracy, learn to critically analyze what they receive from abroad, and write their own opinion pieces in response. PEARL World Youth News Service is a partnership between iEARN and the Daniel Pearl Foundation. Working collaboratively, secondary students from around the world contribute to this online international newspaper. Any student can become a PEARL reporter after finishing an online training and certification course.

Other options suggested by the Asia Society include the following:

- Start an international book club for students and teachers to discuss works by international authors
- Initiate an "I Am Poetry Slam" where students create poetry from their own perspective of children and those from other nations
- Explore contemporary literary genres such as anime or graphic novels from around the world
- Explore the theme of individual and collective identity – a topic of high interest to middle and high school students – using international coming-of-age stories

Why Do We Need to Begin With a School Mission Statement?

Most school mission statements are mushy at best and unrealistic at worst. As blogger Terry Heick states, "a lot is asked of mission statements. They have to sell the school, please the superintendent, and rally the community. Only they read like inscriptions on national monuments or the elegies of fallen heroes." Heick gives the example of the Avenues School:[5]

> We will graduate students who are accomplished in the academic skills one would expect; at ease beyond their borders; truly fluent in a second language; good writers and speakers one and all; confident because they excel in a particular passion; artists no matter their field; practical in the ways of the world; emotionally unafraid and physically fit; humble about their gifts and generous of spirit; trustworthy; aware that their behavior makes a difference in our ecosystem; great leaders when they can be, good followers when they should be; on their way to well-chosen higher education; and, most importantly, architects of lives that transcend the ordinary.

Heick believes that they are all pretty worthless and "would get rid of them" and "replace them with something that parents might say and children might believe in – or even say themselves." The Avenues one is characteristic of a desire to please outsiders and not provide a working vision (apart from the laudatory reference to the need for graduates to be truly bilingual) for the school itself around the idea of graduates working in jobs that require understanding of how to communicate across cultural divides. The problem is that they tend to be wish statements. Even some good ones, Dr. Chris Drew found after reviewing over 70 of them, do not relate to these global realities, with only two that do directly:[6]

> Our vision is to prepare and motivate our students for a rapidly changing world by instilling in them critical thinking skills, a global perspective, and a respect for core values of honesty, loyalty, perseverance, and compassion. Students will have success for today and be prepared for tomorrow.

> We aim to develop well-rounded and thoughtful students prepared to cope with a changing post-modern and globalized world.

They are a notch better in that they are forward-looking action statements to a world that is moving towards becoming more global. The advice from the Asia Society is to work on improving them. They have their use value in many ways; they can serve as the means by which to communicate the schools' core identity and to what extent discretionary activities, such as the use of outside speakers, international festivals, student clubs and societies can contribute.

It is important to emphasize, a mission statement is not useful if it just sits in a metaphorical attic gathering dust. It must be continually discussed and critiqued against current affairs as well as lived out in the practice and instruction of teachers. A principal from a highly praised independent globally minded school in Canada told me that it was important after a series of what were termed "microaggressions" that came following the George Floyd murder by police officials. Following other incidents a black woman graduate wrote a letter to the principal stating that she did not feel that her education at the school "had allowed her and her classmates to learn enough about the history of colonial oppression, injustice and ongoing racism and discrimination in the world today."[7] This all sparked a re-examination of the school's mission statement that could be seen as a generic "Inspiring Excellence in Education and Life" and airily worded vision statement:

> By inspiring excellence – the continuous pursuit of personal best – in education and life, The _ school strives to equip lifelong learners to thrive in a culturally diverse and interdependent world and to embrace, with passion and confidence, their responsibility always to do their best to support others and to make a difference by serving their communities, both locally and in the world at large.

The principal decided to drill down to what they meant by global education – the school set up a Diversity Equity and Inclusion Steering Group that explored in greater depth their core values related to global education. They made the following revisions to their definition (marked in italics).

> Education for global citizenship helps enable young people to develop the core intercultural competencies which allow them to actively engage with the world, locally and internationally, and help to make it a more peaceful, just and sustainable place.
> Global citizenship is not an additional subject, it is an ethos and is values driven. It is best implemented through a whole-school approach, involving everyone from learners themselves to the wider community. It is promoted through the curriculum and other educational experiences in a way that highlights aspects such as social justice, the appreciation of diversity and the importance of sustainable development.

96 *School and Classroom Approaches*

Our understanding of our indigenous cultures, the many cultures represented in our community and other cultures around the world is central to the values and well-being of Canada and all nations.

Why are these conversations important? Because they give everyone (including students who were also involved in this process) a chance to see how words matter and that words sometimes are simply empty if they are not examined and subject to being reviewed and updated as circumstances change. The words that were added, for example to the definition words like "ethos and values driven," are important not because they are high sounding but they go to the issue of the school's very identity. The changes suggest that there is a moral component to the mission that was missing in the past. Similarly the important addition of a whole-school approach eliminates the issue that global education is good for some subjects (social studies and geography) but not others such as science and math.

The changes emerged because discussions were allowed to range far and wide and probed such questions as teachers asking:

What does it mean to be human? (culture, religion, science, world views, knowledge systems, ways of knowing, values, understanding, literacies, numeracies) We need to question our own beliefs and facilitate a safe space to have these conversations and for students to have these conversations with authenticity, intentionality, and self reflection. We need to have space and time to do this on a ground level, not just through policy.

The incidents in question prompted teachers to want more than a superficial approach to this exercise but to really help students understand at a deeper level the seriousness of the issues related to human identity that transcend questions of race. There is also an acknowledgment that some of those discussions must be held in 'safe spaces' and before they do teachers need themselves to examine their own beliefs and prejudices.

How to Overcome Schools' Resistance to Embracing Global Competency

The OECD, through its PISA assessment in 2018 concerning global competency, reports there are some positive associations between various aspects of the school climate and global competency. This association should not surprising as the OECD writes

Schools, in particular, are places where human dignity takes on a concrete meaning, because every student deserves equal justice, equal opportunity and equal dignity.

What we can derive from the latest PISA results concerning global competency is that there seems a high correlation between school culture and performance on PISA's global competency assessment.[8]

Five issues seem to be the most significant:

1. School clubs and societies (such as Model UNs) that give students opportunities to express themselves, particularly those with a global slant make a significant difference.
2. Boys more than girls seem to participate more in out-of-school activities but girls involve themselves in activities related to intercultural understanding and communication.[9]
3. In many countries it is students from immigrant backgrounds that are more globally aware than their non-immigrant peers as well as possessing greater self-efficacy regarding global issues, greater ability to understand different perspectives, higher interest in learning about

other cultures, greater respect for people from other cultures, higher cognitive adaptability and more positive attitudes towards immigrants.[10]

4. Students from low-income families are placed at a disadvantage concerning their ability to be globally competent. What it means is that lack of access to learning opportunities does not result from lack of opportunities in disadvantaged schools, but rather from within-school mechanisms that result in lower engagement among disadvantaged students. Thus, when school curricula, educational practices and materials are developed, educators should keep in mind that not all students are predisposed for global and intercultural learning.
5. Teachers perceived by students as being discriminatory reinforce student negative attitudes.[11]
6. Hosting speakers from other countries enables students to understand their cultures and traditions. This hypothesis is aligned with the results from PISA 2018.[12]

But there is, according to both OECD and Fernando Reimers, very little take up of these ideas. For example, Reimers finds after conducting his own survey that fewer than one-half of respondents offer opportunities to develop global competencies, with only one in four principals reporting that they provided opportunities for students or teachers to travel abroad.[13] Reimers argues that

> to break free from the mental trap that sees the development of global competency as competing with other educational purposes, we need to think anew about the relationships among the different goals of education, understanding that schools were created to achieve ambitious civic purposes and that reconnecting with those purposes can make education more relevant, engaging the imagination and energy of both students and teachers.

Reimers advances what he terms a bottom-up approach: teachers trying to work with and "network with similar groups in other schools or districts working to include this purpose in policies, standards, and curricula or secure resources in support of global education initiatives." More concretely it means town meetings involving parents, teachers as well as business leaders and students themselves to understand how they might best respond to their global futures. They might first map out how dependent their community is on foreign trade – and how many companies that their students will be aspiring to join are in fact multinationals and will be requiring a new set of global skills from their employees. The next step might be to embrace a common cause – a project that might be 'glocal,' combining local and global. It could be something as simple as setting a goal to plant more trees to designing sustainable energy policies for the school and community that would include more car pooling, less use of single-use plastic and even growing vegetables.

It can also start with teachers believing in the fact that the central values of tolerance and understanding and learning from other cultures is not something that can be left to chance but that these need to be taught as part of the implicit curriculum. It also means that principals must budget for professional development directed to just serving the needs of creating a more open and globally aware school community.

What Other Initiatives Can Principals Launch to Advance Global Culture?

Global Certificates

Global certificates provide an incentive to students to really grow their understanding of the world – they can be part of a travel abroad program, service learning or special project that can be awarded by teachers or departments as a capstone project. As the Asia Society reports, some

98 *School and Classroom Approaches*

schools like Providence Day School in Charlotte, North Carolina, offer a Global Studies Diploma in addition to their regular high school diploma

> for hosting an exchange student or participate in a study visit abroad with a home stay; participate in two globally focused events or clubs; complete a global research project; and demonstrate global competency through written global awareness assessments in their senior year.

There are other variations – Needham High School in Needham, Massachusetts, has introduced a new Global Competence Program that allows "students to work toward a Certificate of Global Competence through the successful completion of academic requirements and includes foreign exchange and community service opportunities."

An even more innovative idea comes from The Olathe Kansas School District which after conducting focus groups of more than 400 community participants on the necessary ingredients of a 21st-century education created "21st Century High School" programs that allow students to earn endorsements, much like honors notations on transcripts, for successfully completing programs that augment their 21st-century skills.

What Separates a Course of Study From a Certificate?

What separates 'taking classes' from qualifying for a global certificate program? Most programs require a minimum amount of time or credits spent in globally focused classes, including world language classes, and some require a proficiency exam or a capstone project.

But a quality that all certificate programs share is that students have to research and analyze content as professionals do, and they have to apply the knowledge they learned in real-life contexts. They take action and create change – however big or small – in the real world.

In Illinois, for example, students must analyze information, reach out and work with experts in the field, and apply their learning to a project that creates change. Through this, students synthesize and solidify what they learn and understand as a broader process by which they are not passive bystanders, but rather leaders in effecting change.

Students in Wisconsin must analyze pieces of writing or artwork with a global focus, allowing them to exercise their skills of critical thinking and recognizing other perspectives.

Source: From Global Ed Certificate Program http://globaledcertificate.org/curriculum/

International Days

Most teachers will not find themselves involved in setting school policy but they can learn to exercise their voice. One way is to notice the calendar – there are a plethora of international days to celebrate. Before there were UN international days, there were ways the world community notified its people of its global identity. There are hundreds of days recognized[14] by the United Nations – for example there is the *International Day of Human Rights*, which takes place on December 10. According to the UN,

> This Day is observed all around the world with initiatives ranging from military and police officers swapping guns for running shoes in South Sudan, to a student competition in Russia,

or a exhibit in Brazil. All in all, a multitude of individuals from all walks of life get involved, in a way or another, in the celebration of this special day.

Other most popular days include International Women's Day (March 8), World Water Day (March 22) and the International Day of Peace (September 8). These are all worth bringing to the school's principal or a staff meeting and delegating a student committee to help manage the events and activities that could be organized. In other words teachers should not just hide away in their classrooms and post maps, flags and international posters on the walls – as useful as that might be, they should be proactive in promoting a culture of tolerance and understanding in the school community as well. A first step might be to form a committee to support that kind of effort that would start with, say, a food festival on a day like Cinco de Mayo but would extend to regular celebrations that start to support the regions of the world their school population is drawn from.

Professional Development

One area that professional development can focus on is to assist teachers in creating classroom cultures in which students feel safe to express their opinions, safe to speculate and safe to disagree with their fellow students or even their teacher, without being discourteous. Mieke Van Ingelghem and Dima Bou Mosleh, teacher-educators at University College Leuven-Limburg in Belgium, seek to train teachers to empower learners, enabling them to question and critique what they see in the world. The teacher acts as a facilitator, challenging students to alter their worldviews. "Never stop when a student has given the 'right' answer," Van Ingelghem says. "Always ask if there is another perspective, another point of view, another explanation, another way to solve a problem, to stimulate critical thinking." The Innovative Schools Network supported by OECD in Japan is also trying to encourage students to speak up more and to help teachers get comfortable with them doing so. Hideo Yamada, the director of global education at one of the network schools, the Kaetsu Ariake Junior & Senior High School, wants students to feel that they can "communicate their ideas directly to others, without hesitation, and without hurting anyone." Instead of being the authority on every topic, the teachers are learning to be "learners just like their students," he says. Yamada says the Japanese government is encouraging the changes as part of a larger, national effort to help students become global citizens. Traditionally, he says, Japanese people have not felt a need to engage with people outside their country. Now, however, because of the globalization of the economy and other ways in which nations are becoming more connected, Japan wants its students to become critical thinkers and better able to interact with people from different cultures.

Teaching for Global Competence in a Rapidly Changing World, Asia Society/OECD 2018

Mulgrave School in Vancouver, British Columbia in Canada, was already paying attention to developing global citizens. But, as part of a new five-year strategic plan, the school wanted to do more. "We want our students to be able to lead active lives as international citizens who can move freely in different countries and different cultures," Head of School John Wray says. We want students to "have the skills, values, attitudes, and qualities to survive, thrive, and be happy no matter where they are in the world." Jamie Caton, a third-grade teacher at the Mulgrave School, lived all over the world while growing up and was tapped to join a team seeking certification by the Council of International Schools. The team drew up objectives for developing global competence and for ensuring that everything the school did – including lesson plans, teaching methods, professional-development programs, extracurricular activities, capstone projects, assessments and opportunities for international travel – were aligned with the objectives. "Global competence is not an add-on," Caton says. "It is implicit in every part of the curriculum" from kindergarten on. For example, the school's first graders learning about bees inspected hives at the school, studied the importance of bees in agriculture and learned about the decline in bee populations around the world due to pesticides and pollutants – a way to examine a worldwide problem that was nonetheless developmentally appropriate. "Children from the earliest ages can be thinking critically about everything they are learning in a global context," Caton says. One readily available resource that schools should tap into is the diversity of the students in their classrooms. In many schools, students speak a variety of languages, bring different cultural assets and have international experiences that can enrich discussions and provide alternative perspectives on issues. Another often-underutilized resource is the diversity of the community. Families, local businesses operated by immigrants, cultural organizations, and universities can all help broaden students' understanding of the world.

Eltham High School, in Melbourne, Australia, has been working for eight years to create an academically rigorous, interdisciplinary curriculum for teaching global competence and 21st-century skills. Educators at the school created a school-wide curriculum and an instructional approach aligned with it. Loren Clarke, the head of curriculum, works intensively with three or four teachers from different disciplines at a time to help design specific lessons. The curriculum addresses issues such as sustainability and livability as well as controversial issues such as nuclear power, stem-cell research, world hunger, spending on eradicating AIDS, and the relationship between military spending and poverty. Students are taught to examine both sides of issues and to use evidence to make informed judgments. Although carefully designing a curriculum and planning how to implement it are important, Clarke says it is also important to just get started. "You can spend all your time planning but . . . you won't fully comprehend how it's going to work until you get in there and actually do it," she says. "The more you do it, the more you can refine your plan."

Conclusion

The all-embracing nature of global education, which can be seen either as a set of competencies or just as validly argued as a set of capacities and dispositions, requires a whole-school approach. One teacher working on their own will be far less successful in making the necessary connections for their students than a team of teachers led by an overarching philosophy. This is the value of the International Studies Schools Network (ISSN) created by the Asia Society, a national network of "design-driven public schools that are achieving success in attaining their core mission: to develop college-ready, globally competent high school graduates."[15]

Notes

1. Barth, R. (2006). *Improving schools from within: Teachers, parents, and principals can make the difference*. Jossey Bass, p. 8.
2. PISA 2018 Results (Volume VI), Are Students Ready to Thrive in an Interconnected World?
3. Global human identification and citizenship: A review of psychological studies. *Advances in Political Psychology*, *40*(Suppl. 1), 2019.
4. On average across OECD countries, students reported engaging in about five learning activities at school (the maximum being ten). This number varies substantially between countries and economies. Students in Albania, Baku (Azerbaijan), Colombia, the Dominican Republic, Indonesia, Jordan, Peru,

the Philippines, Singapore and Thailand reported engaging in more than seven activities, while students in France, Hungary, Israel, Latvia, the Russian Federation (hereafter "Russia"), Scotland (United Kingdom) and Slovenia reported engaging in fewer than five.

5. Heick, T., *The problem with most school mission statements*. Retrieved July 19, 2021, from www.teachthought.com/education/school-mission-statement-hogwash/

6. Drew, C. (2019). *79 examples of school vision and mission statements*, October 14. Retrieved July 19, 2021, from https://helpfulprofessor.com/school-vision-and-mission-statements/

7. Personal Interview with Martin Jones, Assistant Head of Mulgrave School, Vancouver, Canada, 12/2/2020.

8. On the scaled index, principals in Belarus, Iceland, Ireland, Poland, Russia, Scotland (United Kingdom), Singapore, Spain, Ukraine and the United Arab Emirates reported the highest levels of positive multicultural beliefs among their teachers, while those in Baku (Azerbaijan), Hong Kong (China), Jordan, Korea, Lebanon, Morocco, Peru, Saudi Arabia, Chinese Taipei and Vietnam reported the lowest levels of these beliefs.

9. For instance, boys were more likely to learn about the interconnectedness of countries' economies, look for news on the Internet or watch the news together during class. They were also more likely to be invited by their teachers to give their personal opinion about international news, to participate in classroom discussions about world events and to analyze global issues together with their classmates. In contrast, girls were more likely than boys to report that they learn how to solve conflicts with their peers in the classroom, learn about different cultures and learn how people from different cultures can have different perspectives on some issues.

10. This finding suggests that a more multicultural background may be more conducive to global and intercultural understanding. Similarly, more multicultural classrooms could create a culturally rich environment that helps both immigrant and native-born students learn about one another. Some of the results align with this hypothesis. In some countries, having more than 10% immigrant students in a school is associated with more positive attitudes towards immigrants. However, this was true only in long-standing immigrant destinations, suggesting that the positive association may be conditional on successful integration policies.

11.
> Students are likely to emulate the behaviour of their teachers. If teachers normalise discrimination and if discrimination becomes an institutional problem, then students may develop discriminatory attitudes towards those who are different from them. By contrast, when teachers do not exhibit discriminatory attitudes and set clear rules about intercultural relations, then students may become aware of what constitutes discriminatory behaviour.

12. In general, having contact with people from other countries at school (and in the family, neighborhood and circle of friends) is positively, weakly to moderately, associated with students' intercultural skills and attitudes towards living with others. The most notable associations were found between having contact with people from other countries at school and students' self-efficacy regarding global issues, cognitive adaptability, interest in learning about other cultures, respect for people from other cultures, ability to understand different perspectives and understanding of intercultural communication.

13. Leading for global competency. *Educational Leadership*, September 2009, Volume 67, Number 1 Teaching for the 21st Century. Retrieved from www.ascd.org/publications/educational-leadership/sept09/vol67/num01/Leading-for-Global-Competency.aspx

14. *United Nations observances*. Retrieved July 19, 2021, from www.un.org/en/observances

15. Hunt, F., & King, R., *Supporting whole school approaches to global learning: Focusing learning and mapping*. Development Education Research Centre for the Global Learning Programme, Research Paper Number 13.

> The network's overarching goal is for every student to graduate with the "knowledge, skills, and habits of mind necessary to succeed in the 21st century global environment" (p. 14).

Afterword

As you spend time reflecting on this book you may wonder if you can truly shift towards becoming a globally minded teacher? As the ancient Chinese proverb has it, a journey of a thousand miles begins with the first step. So the right question to ask is what small steps can I take in the direction of making my classroom more aware of the global context? Why is this so important – book-length important you might ask – it is important because we need a global view of things because our gaze has to shift from seeing our world from an egocentric view to viewing our world as a planetary community. If I had to come up with a visual image of what I think it is needed it is what I term a globalscope. It is my made-up word to describe the opposite of a microscope. Microscopes are useful in many ways – they enlarge our vision so that the teeming life under our fingertips is exposed and we can begin to see bacteria and even cellular life. While microscopes are good at helping us explore the invisible world we inhabit, we need the equivalent for the world that exists way beyond our sight as well. The globalscope is a macro view of the world that can only be possible by viewing items across space and time. Unlike the microscope we cannot position its lens neatly on the surface of a lab or classroom. It has no physical reality – rather it is an imagined state that we want all our students to experience that allows students to see an object, practice or event as the work in one way or another of global forces. Take any of the familiar historic events we discuss in classrooms – the industrial revolution, slavery, the American Civil War, the Holocaust, the Great Depression, etc. and apply the some critical frames that can cultivate a global sensibiliy. Such a critical lens expands students' horizons by (in the words of Asia Society report encouraging students to help in the words of an Asia Society report,[1] "investigate the world beyond their immediate environment by examining issues of local, global, and cultural significance; recognize, understand, and appreciate the perspectives and world views of others; communicate ideas with diverse audiences from the particularities of the 'event's' time and place so that students can understand that these are not events that existed at some point in a remote past – the product of an alien universe peopled by folks in strange costumes but world events, shaped in one form or another by the same kind of global dynamics such as racial ideologies, trade imbalances, population growth and capitalism that continue to inform events today.

An example or two is maybe in order here – as I write, the world's population (depending on where you live) finds itself recovering from what in another century would have been referred to as a plague – the Covid19 pandemic. The pandemic, inflicting what now amounts to millions of deaths around the world, has left countless grieving for the loss of family members and friends, and many more scarred and many traumatized. We will all be trying in various ways to place this experience in some kind of perspective. One of those important perspectives is a global one. A worldview of the pandemic is appropriate since it opens up a span of reactions that are often ignored by the media. What we see when we look both globally and historically is that the tendency to blame others – minorities in particular – has always been one of those knee-jerk reactions. It is hard to forget that our former president referred to Covid as the Chinese flu or

Afterword 103

Kungflu, setting off a chain of anti-Asian violence in the US. When we review the history of the Black Death we see how common it was to blame the Jews for the disease. In the middle of the 14th century, hundreds of Jews in France and Spain were either massacred in the ghettos where they were confined or were murdered in their homes. Some 2,000 Jews were burnt alive on February 14, 1349 in the 'Valentine's Day' Strasbourg massacre, even though the plague had yet to arrive in the city. Just a year before the Strasbourg massacre it is important to know that an alternative response to the enormous suffering was enacted and was documented by the famous traveler Ibn Baṭṭūṭa who was an eyewitness to the coming together of all religions as well as all social classes, writing that after three days of fasting, "the rulers, notables, judges and all different (social) classes gathered in the mosque until it became crowded and they stayed the whole night. Among them were people praying, remembering (God), and calling out (to him)."[8] After the Morning Prayer, they all left together on foot and in their hands were Qur'āns (*al-maṣāḥif*). Among them were the "Jews with their Torahs and the Christians with their Gospels." Everyone was crying, imploring and seeking intercession with God's Books and Prophets."[2]

We can all learn that scapegoating is not inevitable, that we as humans have choices as to how to respond to a plague – either in 14th-century Damascus, Syria as a natural disaster with a plea for God's mercy similar to the way this population had responded to drought – or as in Strasburg and elsewhere in Europe as a form of religiously inspired punishment by a God that had taken religious sides. It was out of place to blame one religion or another for its occurrence. As Mirza argues, the

> Damascus religious authority was able to create a new practice which was based on the precedent of the rain prayer. To order the community to engage in a gathering similar to the rain prayer was not too much of a mental shift and therefore gained wide support and appeal among the population.[3]

The task for the teacher is to help the student understand that human nature does not differ much between countries or between centuries and that the world is full of useful examples that we might or might not choose to follow. So we need the globalscope as a way to escape the cultural blinders that otherwise might trap us and curtail our ability to see the different ways culture shapes us but does not completely define who we are. In teaching with the use of the globalscope it becomes evident that while the old textbook reliance on facts and dates are important we also recognize the need to connect the student's experience with the larger human story. Whether that connection, that flash of recognition that under similar conditions I could react in this way, is triggered by a slave narrative, an extract from a wartime diary or a remembrance of a plague year is immaterial. Our objective is to provide the student space to explore for him- or herself their own sense of human connection with people whenever and wherever they might be situated in space and time. It is the teachers' role to help students understand that these events have no real end. They are constantly studied because they resonate with the times and whether we or they are aware of it are not, we are connected to everyone on the planet.

As the great 19th-century essayist Ralph Waldo Emerson wrote,

> To the young mind, everything is individual, stands by itself. By and by, it finds how to join two things, and see in them one nature; then three, then three thousand; and so, tyrannized over by its own unifying instinct, it goes on tying things together, diminishing anomalies, discovering roots running under ground, whereby contrary and remote things cohere, and flower out from one stem.[4]

We all exist in relation with each other as the physicist Carlo Rovelli remarks, relating our current knowledge of the quantum universe – "everything is what it is only with respect to something else." We are all interconnected and interdependent.[5]

104 *Afterword*

Some new research on tree life suggests that the forest is not some kind of haphazard collection of trees but a genuine organic community. As Peter Wohlleben in the *Secret Lives of Trees* writes,

> Beeches, spruce, and oaks all register pain as soon as some creature starts nibbling on them. When a caterpillar takes a hearty bite out of a leaf, the tissue around the site of the damage changes. In addition, the leaf tissue sends out electrical signals, just as human tissue does when it is hurt. Surprisingly, news bulletins are sent via the roots not only by means of chemical compounds but also by means of electrical impulses that travel at the speed of a third of an inch per second. Once the latest news has been broadcast, all oaks in the area promptly pump tannins through their veins.

In our best moments the world acts like trees in a forest – to protect its own species and to use all the tools at our disposal to fight off common enemies. Too often the world is not pictured this way but rather as a fiercely competitive place where powerful countries and majority populations get to determine the rules of the road and wars are a necessary struggle. But even Darwin, whose name has been falsely connected with the related idea of the survival of the fittest regarded compassion for fellow humans as one of humanity's highest moral achievements. As Eckman writes, Darwin believed that reason

> should make it obvious that individuals should not only be compassionate to strangers in his or her own nation but extend that concern to all peoples, of all nations, and of all races. . . . [E]xperience unfortunately shews [sic] us how long it is before we look at them as our fellow creatures. Sympathy beyond the confines of man, that is humanity to the lower animals, seems to be one of the latest moral acquisitions.[6]

It is time for fellow global educators to write the next chapter concerning mankind's necessary evolution. It has to begin and can only begin in the classroom.

Notes

1. Asia Society, OECD, *Teaching for Global Competence in a Rapidly Changing World*, Retrieved 2018, from https://asiasociety.org/sites/default/files/inline-files/teaching-for-global-competence-in-a-rapidly-changing-world-edu.pdf
2. Strasbourg Massacre. *Wikipedia*. Retrieved from https://en.wikipedia.org/wiki/Strasbourg_massacre
3. Mirza, Y., *"It was a memorable day" – Plague gatherings and their critics*. Retrieved from https://islamiclaw.blog/2020/05/18/younus-y-mirza/
4. *Nature; Addresses and Lectures* by Ralph Waldo Emerson (1849).
5. Banville, J., 'Helgoland' review: The paradox of particles. *Wall Street Journal*, May 28, 2021, Retrieved July 19, 2021, from www.wsj.com/articles/helgoland-review-the-paradox-of-particles-11622231175
6. Ekman, P. (2010). Darwin's compassionate view of human nature. *JAMA*, *303*(6), 557–558 https://doi.org/10.1001/jama.2010.101. Retrieved from https://jamanetwork.com/journals/jama/article-abstract/185330

Appendix One
Global Lesson Plans

Unit Lesson Plans on Climate Change[1]

Global Unit Plan #1 Climate Change	
Central Focus/Context	**Hanvey Domain(s)**
Interdisciplinary Grades 6–12 (Secondary)	State of the planet awareness

Standards

- HS-PS1–2
- HS-ESS3–4
- NC.6.NS.7
- CCSS.MATH.CONTENT.6.SP.B.4
- CCSS.MATH.CONTENT.6.SP.B.5
- CCSS.MATH.CONTENT.6.SP.B.5.A
- CCSS.MATH.CONTENT.6.SP.B.5.B
- CCSS.MATH.CONTENT.6.SP.B.5.C
- LO.3.2.1
- LO.4.1.1
- LO.5.4.1
- LO.5.1.2
- LO.4.1.1.A
- LO.3.1.1.C
- LO.3.3.1
- R.W.9–10.2R.I.9–10.1
- R.I.9–10.7

Objectives/Learning Outcomes

- Students will learn about the greenhouse effect and identify various greenhouse gases
- Students will understand the concept of Global Warming Potential (GWP) and how it will affect our environment if no action is taken
- Students will gain a better understanding of state of the planet awareness, conditions of climate change in various regions
- Students will understand statements of inequality as relative positions of numbers on a number line, and be able to explain these statements in real-world contexts
- Students will develop an emerging awareness of prevailing world conditions in regard to climate change
- Students will determine the mean, median, mode, range, min and max values of a data set

106   *Global Lesson Plans*

Summative Assessments

- Students will write a letter to their pen pals in which they discuss their projects and the issue of climate change

Procedures

Lesson Breakdown

- Lesson 1: The Chemistry of Climate Change
- Lessons 2, 3 and 4: Understanding Air Quality
- Lesson 5: Carbon Footprints around the World
- Lessons 6 and 7: Modeling Climate Change
- Lesson 8: Climate Change at a Global Level

Formative Assessments/Activities

- Hands-on project: students will create a 3D representation of the atmospheric gases and will learn which gases have an impact on the greenhouse effect. Students will also explain the concept of Global Warming Potential and learn about their own impact on climate change by doing the following:

  - Completing the atmospheric gases worksheet
  - Recognizing the greenhouse gases
  - Completing some problems that require students to calculate the amount of carbon dioxide used

- Discussions: students will write, explain, and graph statements of order for rational numbers in a real-world context, in which they write inequality statements about air quality in various cities across the world
- Speakers: students will be here from different non-profit organizations.
- Debate: students will work in groups of two or three and engage in a debate with their fellow classmates on what is considered 'good air quality' and which cities have 'good air quality.' They are to make a list of top ten cities with the best air quality.
- Class work: students will work with their entire class and make a ranking of the top 20 cities around the world with the best air quality based on the AQI Number Line Padlet and the arguments and statements they have engaged in.

Resources

Materials/Technology

- Clean Air Carolina: a non-profit created to ensure that there is cleaner air quality for North Carolina through education and advocacy

  - The Kids Need Clean Air Program
  - AirKeepers Program

- Project Everyone: organization that promotes achieving the objectives of the United Nations' Sustainable Development Goals
- *ePals*: program that allows classrooms around the world to connect with each other
- Air Quality Videos:

  - https://youtu.be/e6rglsLy1Ys
  - https://youtu.be/UU0y38-Bltk
  - https://youtu.be/Xs70ewSdEjE
  - https://youtu.be/JfFXyPWwFhI
  - https://youtu.be/mNZIdHhdQs8
  - https://youtu.be/kUNuHxrd7Y0
  - https://youtu.be/iZKoJTzxeM8

Differentiation (Accommodation/Modification)

- Visual diagrams/aids for all text
- Option to watch videos on air quality

Lesson #1

Objectives	**Standards**
<ul><li>Students will be able to build their own human models of atmospheric gases</li><li>Students will be able to determine which gases are greenhouse gases based upon background information on the greenhouse effect and the role of gases</li><li>Students will be able to understand the concept of Global Warming Potential (GWP)</li><li>Students will be able to relate their understanding of how climate change happens to global climate change issues and begin developing 'state of the planet' awareness</li></ul>	<ul><li>**HS-PS1–2:** Construct and revise an explanation for the outcome of a simple chemical reaction based on the outermost electron states of atoms, trends in the periodic table and knowledge of the patterns of chemical properties</li><ul><li>Students will understand the chemical reactions between greenhouse gases that contribute to climate change</li></ul><li>**HS-ESS3–4:** Evaluate or refine a technological solution that reduces impacts of human activities on climate change and other natural systems</li><ul><li>Students will gain the foundational knowledge to begin the discussion about different ways they can contribute to a reduction of human activities on climate change.</li></ul></ul>

Opening/Hook	**Materials**
Do Now (5 min)<ul><li>Each student will receive a Climate Change Opinions Student Sheet and they will need to circle the option that best represents their opinion</li></ul>Review Do Now (5 min)<ul><li>Students will talk about their answers and why they have that particular opinion. If there is time, I will let one person per group share their answers out loud</li></ul>	Worksheet: *Climate Change Opinions Survey*

Introduction of New Material	
Presentation (10 min)<ul><li>To engage students, I will show an interactive presentation about the chemistry of climate change. During the presentation, the students will be taking notes and participating in discussions.</li><li>Teacher Script: *Today, we will be talking about Global Warming Potential (GWP), which is a measure of how much a given mass of greenhouse gas is estimated to contribute to global warming. This is an important topic to learn because many changes on earth are happening right now due to climate change. It is also crucial to understand how our actions affect the climate environment. Unfortunately, the term 'greenhouses gases' has turned into a political statement rather than a scientific concept. Last week, we learned how chemical reactions occur in our environment and viewed different opinions about climate change. Today, we will learn how chemical reactions affect global warming.*</li><ul><li>Emphasize the lesson's objectives:</li><ul><li>Understanding 'state of the planet' awareness</li><li>Determining which gases are greenhouse gases</li><li>Understanding the concept of Global Warming Potential (GWP)</li></ul></ul></ul>	*Slides*

108 *Global Lesson Plans*

Guided Practice	
Partner Worksheet (20 min): Atmospheric Gases • Students will work in partners to complete the worksheet on atmospheric gases. They are encouraged to use any and all resources available (i.e. computer, textbook, notes) to complete the worksheet. • After completion, review the worksheet as a class and encourage students to correct mistakes.	Worksheet: *Atmospheric Gases*

Independent Practice	
Independent Worksheet (20 min): Real-Life Scenarios • To demonstrate mastery, students will independently complete the worksheet. The objective is for students to understand their own impact on climate change by using the example of CO_2 emissions from a car journey.	Worksheet: *List of Recognized Greenhouse Gases*

Closing	
• The students will complete an exit ticket asking to describe the importance of learning about climate change and what habits they will change in their lives to help the environment. • *Why is it important to learn about climate change?* • *How does climate change affect our everyday lives?* • *What are actions we can take right now to help the environment?*	Exit Ticket • Paper • Digital (Google Form)

Differentiation
• Allow students to work in groups or by themselves during the worksheet portion of the lesson • For the students who have a hard time modeling the molecules using their arms, provide molecular model kits • Provide instructions both verbally and visually • For students who have a hard time doing math, partner them with a student who understands the topic to increase peer-collaboration

Socratic Seminar (Self-Grading)

	5	3	1	*Score (1–5)*
Behavior/Active Listening	Constant eye contact with the speaker. Responding to peer comments. Never needed to ask what question we are on.	Listened, but was occasionally off task. Sometimes needed to be guided back to our question	Did not listen, showed no evidence of listening to classmates. May have also distracted other seminar participants.	

Participation	Participated 5 times without prompting	Participated fewer than 5 times with some prompting	Did not participate	
Understanding of Text	Use of evidence conveyed total familiarity with the text. Always cited page number and article when giving evidence.	Only sometimes used evidence from the text to support their argument.	Did not use evidence from texts to support their points	

Debate Reflection (Teacher and Student) Single Point Rubric

Grows *What did you need to work on?*	Goals Standards	Glows *What did you do really well?*
Student: Teacher:	Students were prepared for the debate with appropriate materials. Students were engaged in conversations. Students demonstrated an ability to think on one's feet. ____/ 25____	Student: Teacher:
Student: Teacher:	Students communicated clearly, concisely, and effectively. Students displayed appropriate behavior during the debate. ____/ 25____	Student: Teacher:
Student: Teacher:	Students provided well-thought-out proposals based on evidence from case studies and/or personal research. Students remained focused on using evidence/data/research for policy reform. ____/ 25____	Student: Teacher:
Student: Teacher:	Students engaged in meaningful discussion with opponents in order to find consensus. ____/ 25____	Student: Teacher:

110　*Global Lesson Plans*

Unit Lesson Plan on Law Enforcement[2]

<table>
<tr><td colspan="2">Global Unit Plan #8
Cross-Cultural Analysis of Law Enforcement</td></tr>
<tr><td>Central Focus/Context</td><td>Hanvey Domain(s)</td></tr>
<tr><td>English 9</td><td>Cross-cultural awareness</td></tr>
<tr><td>Students will explore the differences in outlook and practices amongst various societies as related to law enforcement. Each system of law enforcement will be analyzed through four domains: historical evolution, social context, police institutions and current state of affairs. Students will analyze pieces of text and engage in discussions to highlight similarities and differences between a selected group of countries' law enforcement systems. In the end, students will take what they have learned and propose how the current US system for law enforcement can be improved. Students will have an opportunity to advocate for their position by sending a letter to local government authorities sharing about police reform proposals.</td><td></td></tr>
</table>

Standards

- CCSS.ELA-LITERACY.RI.9–10.1
- CCSS RL.9–10.6
- CCSS SL.9–10.1
- CCSS SL.9–10.3
- CCSS SL.9–10.4

And

Grades 6–12 Literacy in History/Social Studies, Science, & Technical Subjects
www.corestandards.org/ELA-Literacy/RH/11-12/
CCSS.ELA-Literacy.RH.11–12.1
Cite specific textual evidence to support analysis of primary and secondary sources, connecting insights gained from specific details to an understanding of the text as a whole.
CCSS.ELA-Literacy.RH.11–12.2
Determine the central ideas or information of a primary or secondary source; provide an accurate summary that makes clear the relationships among the key details and ideas.
CCSS.ELA-Literacy.RH.11–12.3
Evaluate various explanations for actions or events and determine which explanation best accords with textual evidence, acknowledging where the text leaves matters uncertain.

Objectives/Learning Outcomes

- Students will cite text evidence (in preparing for the class debate)
- Students will draw similarities and differences between different countries and their police (cross-cultural awareness)
- Students will discuss and debate with classmates about a topic
- Students will use evidence to back up their arguments
- Students will present information and demonstrate knowledge by speaking clearly and concisely

Summative Assessments

- Debate: students will be split into two groups (pro-reform and anti-reform) concerning United States law enforcement and will be required to prepare a defense with their group for the upcoming debate. Students will keep in mind that at the end of the debate they must reach consensus about three reforms with the opposing party.

  - USA Reform Coalition: goal should be to implement substantive reforms to how the police operate
  - USA Police Union: goal should be to defend the autonomy of police and ensure funding

Procedures

Lesson Breakdown

- Lesson 1: Introduce unit; explore policing and law enforcement in the United States

  - Opening hook: (Video) *American is not the Greatest Country in the World*

- Lesson 2: Explore law enforcement in Canada
- Lesson 3: Explore law enforcement in Norway
- Lesson 4: Explore law enforcement in Brazil
- Lesson 5: Conversations about police practices with students from another country
- Lesson 6: Develop areas of consensus and disagreement with students from that other country
- Lesson 7: Introduce debate and form groups; research and prepare for debate
- Lesson 8: Debate and post-debate evaluations
- Lesson 9: Write advocacy letter to a US governmental body
- Lesson 10: Role play a UN commission to create a synthesis report that will prioritize the recommendations

Formative Assessments/Activities

- Graphic Organizer: throughout the unit, students will be completing a graphic organizer for four countries. There will be sections for historical evolution of police, social context, police institution and current state of affairs
- Socratic Seminar: students will use dialogue to share concerns and questions about law enforcement in the United States
- Jigsaw Activity: explore articles by breaking down the class into groups. Each group will have an article to analyze and will share their findings to the class
- Group Analysis: in groups, students work together to analyze an article about the four dimensions of the culture of law enforcement in Canada
- Gallery Walk/Independent Reflection: students explore other students' analysis and reflect independently on what they learned
- Independent Journaling: share how initial perceptions of police changes over the course of each lesson; example: summarize and/or highlight the similarities and differences between your original reasons indicated for needing a police service from the beginning of class inside of your classroom journals and your new interpretations based on at least one of the readings from today
- Research Practice: students will practice researching for information using credible and unbiased resources.
- Connect with Another Classroom: CAPSpace (see resources) allows teachers to live stream with another classroom. Connect with a classroom from one of the other countries from the unit. They will watch the class's debate and provide feedback and ask questions. They will also hold their own debate. Our class will watch their debate and draw similarities and differences, ask questions and provide feedback.

Resources

Materials/Technology

- Cultures of Policing Graphic Organizer (see "Additional Materials")
- Article: *TIME – The History of Police in America*
- Article: *The Atlantic: The Culture of Policing is Broken*
- Article: *The Atlantic: Defund the Police*
- Writing Materials (paper/notebook; pencil)
- Socratic Seminar (Self-Grading) Rubric (see "Unit Lesson Plans on Climate Change")
- Video: *Ongoing Protests in Canada Spark Debate over Police Defunding*
- Article: *History of the Royal Canadian Mounted Police (RCMP)*
- Article: *Women in the RCMP*
- Article: *Public Perception of Crime and Justice in Canada: A Review of Opinion Polls*
- Article: *Police Ranks: Breaking Down 8 Different Law Enforcement Positions* (Canada)
- Article: The Guardian – *Canada Urged to Open Its Eyes to Systemic Racism in Wake of Police Violence*
- Article: *Police Resources in Canada*
- Article: *TIME- What the US Can Learn from Countries Where Cops Don't Carry Guns*
- Article: *The Week – What American Can Learn from Nordic Police*
- Article: *PolitiFact – Post Comparing Police Training and Shootings*

112   *Global Lesson Plans*

- Article: *Police Apologize for Harassing Gays*
- Article: *The New York Times – License to Kill: Inside Rio's Record Year of Police Killings*
- Website: *Brazil's Ongoing Domestic Migrations*
- Article: *Brazil Gun Laws*
- Article: *Is Brazil's Military Police Training Too Brutal?*
- Article: *BBC – Rio Violence: Police Killings Reach Record High in 2019*
- Video: Newsroom (TV Show): *America Is Not the Greatest Country in the World*
- *CAPSpace* – Connect with another classroom across the world

Notes

1. Thanks are due to Jia Lin, Camille Goering, Nathalie Villanueva, Ashima Gauba, Elspeth Grasso who created this lesson plan while attending my course on Introduction to Global Education Policy, at Johns Hopkins University. These lesson plans were created with contributions from my Johns Hopkins University Graduate students, those students included Camille Goering, Amanda Palmer, Juliana Mae Neves, Vanessa Morales, Ian Collis, Louisa Christen, Sonia Fantz, Kathleen Sears, Nathalie Villanueva, Ashima Gauba, Elspeth Grasso, Jia Lin.
2. Thanks are due to Juliana Mae Neves, Louisa Christen, Sonia Fantz, Kathleen Sears, Vanessa Moralles and Ian Collis who created this lesson plan while attending my course on Introduction to Global Education Policy, at Johns Hopkins University.

Selective Bibliography

Asia Society. (n.d.). *What is global competence?* Retrieved April 27, 2021, from https://asiasociety.org/education/what-global-competence

Bignold, W., & Gayton, W. (Eds.). (2009). *Global issues and comparative education* (Perspectives in Education Studies Series). Los Angeles, CA: Learning Matters.

Boix Mansilla, V., & Jackson, A. (2011). *Educating for global competence: Preparing our youth to engage the world*. New York: Asia Society.

Bourn, D. (Ed.). (2018). *Debates on global skills: Understanding global skills for 21st century professions* (pp. 87–109). London: Palgrave McMillan.

Brown, S. C., & Kysilka, M. L. (2008). *What every teacher should know about multicultural and global education*. Boston, MA: Pearson.

Gaudelli, W. (2016). *Global citizenship education: Everyday transcendence*. New York: Routledge.

GENE. (2018). Global education in Europe: Concepts, definitions and aims. *GENE*. Retrieved April 27, 2021, from http://gene.eu/wp-content/uploads/GENE-policy-briefing-Concepts-Definitions-for-web.pdf

Ghosh, A. (2016). *The great derangement: Climate change and the unthinkable*. Berkeley: University of Chicago Press.

Goren, H., & Yemini, M. (2017). Global citizenship education redefined: A systematic review of empirical studies on global citizenship education. *International Journal of Educational Research, 82*, 170–183.

Klein, J. (2017). *The global education guidebook: Humanizing K-12 classrooms worldwide through equitable partnerships*. Solution Tree.

Lehtomäki, E., Moate, J., & Posti-Ahokas, H. (2019). Exploring global responsibility in higher education students' cross-cultural dialogues. *European Educational Research Journal, 18*(1).

OECD and Asia Society. (2018). *Teaching for global competence in a rapidly changing world*. Paris: OECD. Retrieved April 27, 2021, from https://asiasociety.org/sites/default/files/inline-files/teaching-for-global-competence-in-a-rapidly-changing-world-edu.pdf

Reimers, F. (2017). *Empowering students to improve the world in sixty lessons*. Charleston, SC: CreateSpace.

Suarez-Orozoco, M. (Ed.). (2007). *Learning in the global era: International perspectives on globalization and education*. Berkeley: University of California Press.

UNESCO. (2017). *Education for people and planet* (Global Education Monitoring Report). Paris: UNESCO.

Wilkerson, I. (2020). *Caste: The origins of our discontent*. New York: Random House.

Zhao, Y. (2017). *Imagining the future of global education: Dreams and nightmares*. New York: Routledge.

Appendix Two
Immigration

Immigration has risen to the top of the global agenda. Climate change, economic pressures, terrorism and increasing civil disorder in many states means that immigration mostly from poor countries to rich ones and from the Global South to the Global North will continue to increase. Students need to be prepared for the kinds of debates and inevitable tensions that will occur in many advanced societies such as the US and most of Europe where a double standard exists. Students should understand how in these societies, as Harari explains, immigration depends on two principles – in return for limited citizenship (usually just the right to work) the immigrant must embrace the values of the host country – which sometimes means giving up some traditional customs. If the immigrant agrees to be a law-abiding citizen and support him- or herself and his or her family there is an expectation that after a length of years they and their children will be given a path to full citizenship.

So as Harari further points out, several debates arise from this set of principles – but before going to the debate format, it is important to humanize this discussion, and no better way of doing that is to review the following video made by the National Academy of Sciences: https://thesciencebehindit.org/how-does-immigration-affect-the-u-s-economy/

Debate 1: Is accepting an immigrant into the country a duty or a favor? The range of opinions span from the host country should accept everyone who applies and the host country should only select the few who bring with them advanced skills in demand by the US or world economy. While the hard core group of anti-immigrants ignores the historic right of refugees fleeing persecution, it also tends to overlook how illegal immigration and or temporary agricultural workers are used by large sectors of the agricultural and building industries and keep prices in those sectors low, since one thing these sectors often don't do is to provide minimum wages or benefits.

Debate 2: Should immigrants be forced to adopt the culture or beliefs of the host country? If they come from cultures that are, for example, intolerant of gays, are they allowed to express their prejudices in their businesses or their churches?

Debate 3: How long should an immigrant wait before being granted full citizenship and should that right be passed down to his or her children?

Debate 4: Are immigrants duty bound to assimilate and leave their traditional customs behind?

At the heart of all these debates is the question, as Yuuval states, whether "all cultures are inherently equal, or do we think some cultures might well be superior to others?" There is a skepticism about people, whether they are claiming to be fleeing persecution or coming because they believe they will do better economically in the host country. We should address this and offer students to view the issue of what immigrants actually offer to the country and how the US, with its relatively open immigration policy until recently, gains economically as a result from its very liberal immigration policies.

Let them view this excellent video made by the National Academy: https://thesciencebehindit. org/how-does-immigration-affect-the-u-s-economy/

114 *Immigration*

Selective Bibliography

Sherman, A., Trisi, D., Stone, C., Gonzales, S., & Sharon Parrott. (2019). *Immigrants Contribute Greatly to U.S. Economy, Despite Administration's "Public Charge" Rule Rationale.* Retrieved April 27, 2021, from www.cbpp.org/research/poverty-and-inequality/immigrants-contribute-greatly-to-us-economy-despite-administrations

Nunn, R., O'Donnell, J., Shambaugh, J. (2018). *A Dozen Facts about Immigration.* Retrieved April 27, 2021, from www.brookings.edu/research/a-dozen-facts-about-immigration/

Hirschman, C. (2013). The contributions of immigrants to American culture. *Daedalus, 142*(3). doi: 10.1162/DAED_a_00217.

Soccer

Exploring Abusive Labor Practices

Teaching Idea/Activity

Ask pairs of students to suggest some possible objection to the view that American culture is a dominant influence across the globe.

Ask the class to rank objections in order of their importance before introducing the ideas to follow.

In order to enable students to appreciate the inadequacies of the cultural imperialists' position, we should familiarize them with the main objections that are frequently raised, whilst acknowledging that these objections are also open to criticism and debate. These objections can be described as follows:

1. The import of cultural products simply increases the range available to people rather than driving out the local equivalents. Indonesian taxi drivers may well listen to the latest American hits on their radios but they may also listen to home-grown music.
2. Imported cultural products are certainly not always American; think of pizzas and British football. And, in New York, or London, you are never too far way from a Chinese restaurant or sushi bar.
3. Many multinational corporations based in America are foreign-owned:

    Random House, for example, is in the hands of Germany's Bertelsmann; Japan's Sony owns Columbia; and France's Vivendi controls Universal Studios.

4. Watching a Hollywood movie or eating a McDonald's burger does not threaten individuals' cultural identities, deeply rooted as they are in their family and immediate social backgrounds; the idea that a coke will change your life is only an advertising slogan.
5. Local cultures may be strengthened by cultural globalization originating in America. Thus, in India, satellite TV has led to an increase in the number of regional channels – channels that carry Indian content.
6. Paradoxically, powerful cultural influences from outside local communities may lead local people to hold on to their own culture with greater determination in reaction to perceived external threats.

Teaching Idea/Activity

Ask students to draw any similarities between the objections listed earlier and the ones they identified.

Ask pairs of students to prepare an introduction to one of the ideas presented previously, suitable for 11-year-old children.

Glocal

Glocal integrates three dimensions of knowing, acting and being and connecting them around a local project. Students can benefit from connecting personal choices related to their local community and how those personal choices relate to global challenges in the wider world.

Glocal projects are long term, individual and passion driven. We live in a world where our actions – whether to choose a gas-guzzling SUV over a hybrid or electric car, or to plan to fly to see the penguins at the southernmost tip of South America or to use single-use containers instead of recycling – have consequences for ourselves, our communities and for the planet. This has spawned the need for the word 'glocal,' a gift to global educators. We can do something that Dewey asks us to do more of in education – start from the child's own experience and work backwards to see how that experience is intrinsically global. The following are some examples:

1. Students taking photos of their own homes or schools and comparing them (using Google maps or other web photos) with counterparts in other countries. What differences do they note? What about the neighborhoods these places are situated in? How do they compare? What can you deduce from these differences?
2. How does climate change affect your local community? Farmers for example are particularly affected by changes in rain patterns, rising temperatures, etc. Talk to people who grow food for a living or even speak to gardeners. What have they experienced? What are they doing about it? What do they want others to do about it including local, state or federal or the UN to do about it?
3. Can anything be done locally when national governments have chosen for one reason or another not to act? What are the communities listed on the website *We Are Still In* doing? And what success are they having? Which projects might be replicated in your local community?

Using Literature

Exploring Gender and Society

After reading Azadeh Moaveni's memoir *Lipstick Jihad* (set in the United States and Iran), students can compare the experience of gender discrimination with Nathaniel Hawthorne's *The Scarlet Letter* and write about the perceptions of women by religious societies. For further reading *I am Malala* by Christina Lamb and Malala Yousafzai is a powerful testament to courage as Malala was shot by extremists simply for being female and wanting to attend school.

Fairy Tales Around the World

We are all familiar with the Cinderella story but how many students know that the Cinderella story has as many as 500 different versions that date back further than Charles Perrault, whose story captured the imagination of countless millions of young readers. Some of the differences are captured in the KidWorld Book *The Cinderella Story Around the World* (https://kidworldcitizen. org/cinderella-story-around-the-world/). There are a series of books that are fascinating for kids to read including *Gingerbread Men Type Stories*, and the *Little Red Riding Hood Multicultural Stories*.

Myths

Tenth graders at Signature Charter School in Evanston, Indiana, "explore the universality of myth, read such texts as Joseph Campbell's *Hero of a Thousand Faces*, the Rubaiyat of Omar Khayyam, the Qur'ān, *Antigone* (by Sophocles) and *The Stranger* (by Albert Camus)."

116 *Immigration*

International Newspapers

At the College of Staten Island High School for International Studies in New York City, teachers and students have created an international newspaper as an authentic writing venue for students and as an opportunity to work with 'colleague' students overseas. At Henry Street School for International Studies, also in New York City, students interview journalists about the international aspects of their profession. Paired readings can show the development of similar writing styles, motifs or character development.

Going Glocal

Tatiana Popa, an English teacher at the largest and oldest high school in Moldova in Eastern Europe, recognized that Chisinau, the capital of Moldova and the city where Popa teaches had a garbage problem when the local dump closed. She had her students engage with students from other countries to explore possible solutions. This helped practice both their English and their problem-solving skills. It also enabled them to "know that their classroom, their school, and their community are all connected with the world and that they are citizens of the world," she says, "and citizens of the world try to make it a better place to live in."[1]

Note

1. *Teaching global competence in a rapidly changing world.* Asia Society and OECD.

Appendix Three

Some Sample Global Lesson Plans

Global Unit Plan #1 Climate Change	
Central Focus/Context Interdisciplinary Grades 6–12 (Secondary)	**Hanvey Domain(s)** State of the Planet Awareness

Standards

- HS-PS1–2
- HS-ESS3–4
- NC.6.NS.7
- CCSS.MATH.CONTENT.6.SP.B.4
- CCSS.MATH.CONTENT.6.SP.B.5
- CCSS.MATH.CONTENT.6.SP.B.5.A
- CCSS.MATH.CONTENT.6.SP.B.5.B
- CCSS.MATH.CONTENT.6.SP.B.5.C
- LO.3.2.1
- LO.4.1.1
- LO.5.4.1
- LO.5.1.2
- LO.4.1.1.A
- LO.3.1.1.C
- LO.3.3.1
- R.W.9–10.2R.I.9–10.1
- R.I.9–10.7

Objectives/Learning Outcomes

- Students will learn about the greenhouse effect and identify various greenhouse gases.
- Students will understand the concept of Global Warming Potential (GWP) how it will affect our environment if no action is taken.
- Students will gain a better understanding of state of the planet awareness, conditions of climate change in various regions.
- Students will understand statements of inequality as relative positions of numbers on a number line, and be able to explain these statements in real-world contexts.
- Students will develop an emerging awareness of prevailing world conditions in regard to climate change.
- Students will determine the mean, median, mode, range, min and max values of a data set.

Summative Assessments

- Students will write a letter to their pen pals in which they discuss their projects and the issue of climate change.

118   *Some Sample Global Lesson Plans*

Procedures

Lesson Breakdown

- Lesson 1: The Chemistry of Climate Change
- Lessons 2, 3, & 4: Understanding Air Quality
- Lesson 5: Carbon Footprints around the World
- Lesson 6 & 7: Modeling Climate Change
- Lesson 8: Climate Change at a Global Level

Formative Assessments/Activities

- Hands-on Project: Students will create a 3D representation of the atmospheric gases and will learn which gases have an impact on the greenhouse effect. Students will also explain the concert of Global Warming Potential and learn about their own impact upon climate change by doing the following:
  - completing the atmospheric gases worksheet
  - recognizing the greenhouse gases
  - completing some problems that requires students to calculate the amount of carbon dioxide used
- Discussions: Students will write, explain, and graph statements of order for rational numbers in a real-world context, in which they write inequality statements about air quality in various cities across the world.
- Speakers: Students will be here from different non-profit organizations.
- Debate; Students will work in groups of two or three and engage in a debate with their fellow classmates on what is considered "good air quality" and which cities have "good air quality." They are to make a list of top ten cities with the best air quality.
- Class Work: students will work with their entire class and make a ranking of the top 20 cities around the world with the best air quality based on the AQI Number Line Padlet and the arguments and statements they have engaged in.

Resources

Materials/Technology

- Clean Air Carolina: a non-profit created to ensure that there is cleaner air quality for North Carolina through education and advocacy

  - The Kids Need Clean Air Program
  - AirKeepers Program

- Project Everyone: organization that promotes achieving the objectives of the United Nations' Sustainable Development Goals
- *ePals*: program that allows classrooms around the world to connect with each other
- Air Quality Videos:

  - https://youtu.be/e6rglsLy1Ys
  - https://youtu.be/UU0y38-Bltk
  - https://youtu.be/Xs70ewSdEjE
  - https://youtu.be/JfFXyPWwFhI
  - https://youtu.be/mNZIdHhdQs8
  - https://youtu.be/kUNuHxrd7Y0
  - https://youtu.be/iZKoJTzxeM8

Differentiation (Accommodation/Modification)

- Visual diagrams/aids for all text
- Option to watch videos on air quality

Some Sample Global Lesson Plans 119

Lesson #

Objectives	**Standards**

• Students will be able to build their own human models of atmospheric gases.
• Students will be able to determine which gases are greenhouse gases based upon background information on the greenhouse effect and the role of gases.
• Students will be able to understand the concept of Global Warming Potential (GWP).
• Students will be able to relate their understanding of how climate change happens to global climate change issues and begin developing "State of the Planet" Awareness
	• **HS-PS1–2:** Construct and revise an explanation for the outcome of a simple chemical reaction based on the outermost electron states of atoms, trends in the periodic table, and knowledge of the patterns of chemical properties.
	
	  • Students will understand the chemical reactions between greenhouse gases that contribute to climate change.
	
	• **HS-ESS3–4:** Evaluate or refine a technological solution that reduces impacts of human activities on climate change and other natural systems.
	
	  • Students will gain the foundational knowledge to begin the discussion about different ways they can contribute to a reduction of human activities on climate change.

Opening/Hook	**Materials**
Do Now (5 min) • Each student will receive a Climate Change Opinions Student Sheet and they will need to circle the option that best represents their opinion. Review Do Now (5 min) • Students will talk about their answers and why they have that particular opinion. If there is time, I will let one person per group share their answers out-loud	Worksheet: *Climate Change Opinions Survey*

Introduction of New Material	

Presentation (10 min)
• To engage students, I will show an interactive presentation about the chemistry of Climate Change. During the presentation, the students will be taking notes and participating in discussions.
• *Teacher Script: Today, we will be talking about Global warming potential (GWP) which is a measure of how much a given mass of greenhouse gas is estimated to contribute to global warming. This is an important topic to learn because many changes on earth are happening right now due to climate change. It is also crucial to understand how our actions affect the climate environment. Unfortunately, the term "greenhouses gases" has turned into a political statement rather than a scientific concept. Last week, we learned how chemical reactions occur in our environment and viewed different opinions about Climate Change. Today, we will learn how chemical reactions affect global warming.*
• Emphasize the lesson's objectives:
 	
  • Understanding "State of the Planet" Awareness
  • Determining which gases are greenhouse gases
  • Understanding the concept of Global Warming Potential (GWP)
	Slides

120 *Some Sample Global Lesson Plans*

Guided Practice	
Partner Worksheet (20min): Atmospheric Gases • Students will work in partners to complete the worksheet on atmospheric gases. They are encouraged to use any and all resources available (i.e. computer, textbook, notes) to complete the worksheet. • After completion, review the worksheet as a class and encourage students to correct mistakes.	*Worksheet: Atmospheric Gases*

Independent Practice	
Independent Worksheet (20min): Real Life Scenarios • To demonstrate mastery, students will independently complete the worksheet. The objective is for students to understand their own impact on climate change by using the example of CO2 emissions from a car journey.	*Worksheet* *List of Recognized Greenhouse Gases*

Closing	
• The students will complete an exit ticket asking to describe the importance of learning about climate change and what habits they will change in their lives to help the environment. • *Why is it important to learn about climate change?* • *How does climate change affect our everyday lives?* • *What are actions we can take right now to help the environment?*	Exit Ticket • Paper • Digital (Google Form)

Differentiation
• Allow students to work in groups or by themselves during the worksheet portion of the lesson. • For the students who have a hard time modeling the molecules using their arms, provide molecular model kits. • Provide instructions both verbally and visually. • For students who have a hard time doing math, partner them with a student who understands the topic to increase peer-collaboration.

Global Unit Plan # 9 **Resources and Equity Issues Around the World**	
Central Focus/Subjects	**Hanvey Domain(s)**
Algebra I (9th grade)	State of the planet awareness
Using mathematical concepts like inequality, rate, linear equations and graphing to explore inequity. By discussing inequity, students develop their global citizenship as well as their empathy towards others.	

Standards

- CCSS.MATH.CONTENT.HSA.REI.A.1
- CCSS.MATH.CONTENT.HSA.REI.A.2

Objectives/Learning Outcomes

- Allocate there are different types of inequality
- Present a concise but persuasive argument based on research
- Explore the impact inequality can have on the wider society and economy
- Practice global perspectives such as cross-cultural awareness, empathy and global dynamics, and apply to global competence by math strategy
- Utilize linear equation by presenting it in graphs and tables
- Decode word problems and identify dependent and independent variables and present them on the x and y-axis

Summative Assessments

- Graphing Linear Equations – Income Inequality Scenarios

Procedures

Lesson Breakdown

- Lesson 1: Introduce global inequality from a mathematical perspective
- Lesson 2: Develop the understanding of global inequality, illustrate minimum wage
- Lesson 3: Practice minimum wage into problem-solving of global inequality.

Formative Assessments/Activities

- True/False Activity: students will guess if statements about global wealth, economic inequality and unemployment are true or false.
  - Example: The 85 richest people in the world have as much wealth as the poorest half of mankind. true. (*Data Source*)
- Ten Chairs of Global Inequality Game: students will explore scenarios of inequality
- Calculate Income: students will complete the rate of pay charts and use the charts to graph basic linear equations.
- Video: *If the World Was Only 100 People*
- Practice Graphing Linear Equations – Income Inequality Scenarios

Resources

Materials/Technology

Article – *The Guardian: 85 Richest People in the World*
Website – *Inequality.org*
Website – *Desmos.com*
Website – *The Guardian: US Employment*
Website – *The World Bank: Proportion of seat held by women in national parliaments*
Video: *If the World was Only 100 People*
Website – *Kids Boost Immunity*
PowerPoint; Handouts; Posters
Calculator
Pencils; Colored Pencils
Ruler

Differentiation (Accommodation/Modification)

122 *Some Sample Global Lesson Plans*

Lesson #1 Global Inequality From a Mathematical Perspective	
Objectives	**Standards**
• Students will be able to define global inequality and global awareness • Students will begin to understand how global inequality operates • Students will begin to understand mathematical concepts of inequality	• CCSS.MATH.CONTENT.HSA.REI.A.: Explain each step in solving a simple equation as following from the equality of numbers asserted at the previous step, starting from the assumption that the original equation has a solution. Construct a viable argument to justify a solution method. • CCSS.MATH.CONTENT.HSA.REI.A.2: Solve simple rational and radical equations in one variable, and give examples showing how extraneous solutions may arise.
Opening/Hook	**Materials**
Hook Activity (5 min): True/False Trivia • True or False question on the theme of world inequality as a warm-up activity. The goal is for students to get engaged in the material and come to the realization that inequality happens in real life.	PowerPoint Ture or False Question: • The 85 richest people in the world have as much wealth as the poorest half of mankind. (true) • In the USA, the average worth of white households in 2009 was $113,149 compared to African American households at $5,677 and Hispanic households at $6,325. (true) • In the UK the unemployment rate for people aged 16–24 is 14.4%. The overall unemployment rate is 5.7%. (true) • Globally, women occupy less than a 25% of all seats in parliament. (true)
Introduction of New Material	

Introduction (5 min)
 	
• Provide students a brief overview of what they will learn in this class through class session outcomes (objectives). The class agenda allows students to clarify the arrangement of the entire course. In this way, students can clearly know what they should do next in class.
• Key Points/Terms to Review
  • Global awareness
  • Global inequality
	Teacher would ask, "when we talk about 'equality,' what does it mean to you?"

Some Sample Global Lesson Plans   123

Guided Practice	
Interactive Game (40 min): Ten Chairs of Global Inequality • Ten Chairs of Global Inequality is the core of this activity. Teachers will utilize the concept of mathematics to introduce the topic of social inequality, such as "each chair does not register 10% of the wealth in the world and each person does not register 10% of the people in the world." Then, we guide students to bring in their own experiences, to choose different countries to play their roles. • In the group discussion stage, students can use mathematical thinking, interdisciplinary thinking to develop their creativity and problem-solving skills. Step 1: Divide the students into groups of 10 and invite the rest of the students to line up at the front of the room, seated in 10 chairs facing the rest of the group. Step 2: Each chair represents 10% of the wealth in the world and each person represents 10% of the people in the world. So, we assume that when one person is in each chair the wealth is shared equally. Step 3: Explain that wealth is what you own: • Your toys – child and adult-types • Your TV, Walkman, iPod, computer • Your clothes • The food in your cupboards • Your family's apartment or house and all the furniture in it • Your family's car or cars • Your cash, bank accounts and savings – in piggy banks or banking institutions Step 4: Explain that wealth like this helps you get other things in life like: • An education Step 5: Create scenarios in which there is an unequal distribution of wealth amongst participants (*see directions*). Ask for students to reflect on how they *feel* during each round and connections they can make to global issues of inequality.	10 + Chairs; World Map; Handouts; Pencils/Pen; Directions: *10 Chairs of Global Inequality*
Independent Practice	
Individual Exploration (10 min) • Provide students with online software to practice the concepts of mathematical equations and inequalities, laying the groundwork for the next two lessons on equations. • The Equality Explorer has different levels of operation options and detailed descriptions.	List materials Laptop/iPad *Equality Explorer: Legends of Learning Website*

124 *Some Sample Global Lesson Plans*

Closing	
Reflection Question (5 min) • Students will answer: *Why do you think global inequality exists?* • Because this is the first chapter of the unit, the overall goal of today's lesson is getting them to be aware of global inequality, before diving into the mathematical concepts related to global inequality.	Exit Ticket • Paper • Digital (Google Form)

Global Unit Plan #8 Cross-Cultural Analysis of Law Enforcement	
Central Focus/Context English 9 Students will explore the differences in outlook and practices amongst various societies as related to law enforcement. Each system of law enforcement will be analyzed through four domains: historical evolution; social context; police institutions; and current state of affairs. Students will analyze pieces of text and engage in discussions to highlight similarities and differences between a selected group of countries' law enforcement systems. In the end, students will take what they have learned and propose how the current US system for law enforcement can be improved. Students will have an opportunity to advocate for their position by sending a letter to local government authorities sharing about police reform proposals.	**Hanvey Domain(s)** Cross-Cultural Awareness

Standards
• CCSS.ELA-LITERACY.RI.9–10.1   • CCSS RL.9–10.6   • CCSS SL.9–10.1   • CCSS SL.9–10.3   • CCSS SL.9–10.4   And   Grades 6–12 Literacy in History/Social Studies, Science, & Technical Subjects   www.corestandards.org/ELA-Literacy/RH/11-12/   *CCSS.ELA-Literacy.RH.11–12.1*   Cite specific textual evidence to support analysis of primary and secondary sources, connecting insights gained from specific details to an understanding of the text as a whole.   *CCSS.ELA-Literacy.RH.11–12.2*   Determine the central ideas or information of a primary or secondary source; provide an accurate summary that makes clear the relationships among the key details and ideas.   *CCSS.ELA-Literacy.RH.11–12.3*   Evaluate various explanations for actions or events and determine which explanation best accords with textual evidence, acknowledging where the text leaves matters uncertain.

Objectives/Learning Outcomes

- Students will cite text evidence (in preparing for the class debate).
- Students will draw similarities and differences between different countries and their police (Cross-Cultural Awareness).
- Students will discuss and debate with my classmates about a topic.
- Students will use evidence to back up my arguments.
- Students will present information and demonstrate knowledge by speaking clearly and concisely.

Summative Assessments

- Debate: Students will be split into two groups (pro-reform and anti-reform) concerning United States' Law Enforcement and will be required to prepare a defense with their group for the upcoming debate. Students will keep in mind that at the end of the debate they must reach consensus about 3 reforms with the opposing party.

  - USA Reform Coalition: goal should be to implement substantive reforms to how the police operate
  - USA Police Union: goal should be to defend the autonomy of police and ensure funding

Procedures

Lesson Breakdown

- Lesson 1: Introduce unit; explore policing and law enforcement in the United States

  - Opening Hook: (Video) *American is not the Greatest Country in the World*

- Lesson 2: Explore law enforcement in Canada
- Lesson 3: Explore law enforcement in Norway
- Lesson 4: Explore law enforcement in Brazil
- Lesson 5: Conversations about police practices with students from another country
- Lesson 6: Develop areas of consensus and disagreement with students from that other country
- Lesson 7: Introduce debate and form groups; research and prepare for debate
- Lesson 8: Debate and post-debate evaluations
- Lesson 9: Write advocacy letter to a US governmental body
- Lesson 10: Role play a UN commission to create a synthesis report that will prioritize the recommendations

Formative Assessments/Activities

- Graphic Organizer: Throughout the unit, students will be completing a graphic organizer for four countries. There will be sections for historical evolution of police, social context, police institution, and current state of affairs
- Socratic Seminar: Students will use dialogue to share concerns and questions about law enforcement in the United States.
- Jigsaw Activity: Explore articles by breaking down the class into groups. Each group will have an article to analyze and will share their findings to the class.
- Group Analysis: In groups, students work together to analyze an article about the four dimensions of the culture of law enforcement in Canada.
- Gallery Walk/Independent Reflection: Students explore other students' analysis and reflect independently on what they learned.
- Independent Journaling: Share how initials perceptions of police changes over the course of each lesson; Example: Summarize and/or highlight the similarities and differences between your original reasons indicated for needing a police service from the beginning of class inside of your classroom journals and your new interpretations based on at least one of the readings from today
- Research Practice: Students will practice researching for information using credible and unbiased resources.
- Connect with Another Classroom: CAPSpace (see resources) allows teachers to live stream with another classroom. Connect with a classroom from one of the other countries from the unit. They will watch our class' debate and provide feedback and ask questions. They will also hold their own debate. Our class will watch their debate and draw similarities and differences, ask questions, and provide feedback.

126 *Some Sample Global Lesson Plans*

Resources
Materials/Technology • Cultures of Policing Graphic Organizer (see below) • Article: *TIME – The History of Police in America* • Article: *The Atlantic: The Culture of Policing is Broken* • Article: *The Atlantic: Defund the Police* • Writing Materials (Paper/Notebook; Pencil) • Socratic Seminar (Self-Grading) Rubric (see below) • Video: *Ongoing Protests in Canada Spark Debate over Police Defunding* • Article: *History of the Royal Canadian Mounted Police (RCMP)* • Article: *Women in the RCMP* • Article: *Public Perception of Crime and Justice in Canada: A Review of Opinion Polls* • Article: *Police Ranks: Breaking Down 8 Different Law Enforcement Positions* (Canada) • Article: The Guardian – *Canada Urged to Open its Eyes to Systemic Racism in Wake of Police Violence* • Article: *Police Resources in Canada* • Article: *TIME- What the US Can Learn from Countries Where Cops Don't Carry Guns* • Article: *The Week- What American Can Learn From Nordic Police* • Article: *PolitiFact -Post Comparing Police Training and Shootings* • Article: *Police Apologize for Harassing Gays* • Article: *The New York Times – License to Kill: Inside Rio's Record Year of Police Killings* • Website: *Brazil's Ongoing Domestic Migrations* • Article: *Brazil Gun Laws* • Article: *Is Brazil's Military Police Training Too Brutal?* • Article: *BBC – Rio Violence: Police Killings Reach Record High in 2019* • Video: Newsroom (TV Show): *America is not the Greatest Country in the World* • *CAPSpace* – Connect with another classroom across the world;

Differentiation (Accommodation/Modification)

Lesson #1	
Objectives	**Standards**
• Students will begin to analyze the current state of US policing. • Students will begin to form critical observations of the US, both in general and specifically towards policing practices. • Students will become familiar with the graphic organizer they will use throughout the unit to collect observations. • Students will understand the overview of the unit and each lesson.	**CCSS SL.9–10.1** Initiate and participate effectively in a range of collaborative discussions (one-on-one, in groups and teacher-led) with diverse partners on grades 9–10 topics, texts and issues, building on others' ideas and expressing their own clearly and persuasively

Opening/Hook (10 min)	Materials
Hook (5 min) • Students enter the classroom, grab their notebooks and sit at their desk. To engage students and capture their interest, we will watch the video clip from the *Newsroom*, "America Is Not the Greatest Country" and view images of the Black Lives Matter mural in front of the White House. • *"What is this about?"* Students have 5 minutes to write down anything that comes to mind, to write their perceptions of the cause, movement and demands. **Opening (5 min):** • Ask 5 students to share something they wrote down and write key phrases on the board (e.g. police brutality, George Floyd, reform, defund the police, systemic racism, etc.) • Communicate that students are beginning a mini unit on policing and policing cultures around the world. Ask students why they think it is an important issue, and then communicate that we are at a historic tipping point where there is more attention and public consensus than ever that something needs to change, and that they have a chance to decide whether or not to play a role and what role to play. • To connect to previous lessons, highlight the main standards (citing evidence to analyze texts, to explore texts from a point of view) and how they apply to the ability to participate in productive discussions in civic society.	https://www.youtube.com/watch?v=bIpKfw17-yY
Introduction of New Material (5 min)	
• Show students a roadmap of our unit and our 6 lessons with three country studies, one research day and our end-of-unit final debate on reform. • Emphasize that the purpose of our comparison is to learn whether our problems are unique to the United States and compare how other countries structure and train their police departments, and what we can learn from them. To do this, we will be keeping a graphic organizer. • Explain that students will be collaborating with a school in Brazil going through the same unit, and that the final day will be a debate worth a significant grade that is live-streamed to our Brazilian colleagues.	PowerPoint slides: Roadmap Graphic organizer for four countries with columns for historical evolution of police, social context, police institution and current state of affairs Cards with Team A and Team B that students pick randomly

128 *Some Sample Global Lesson Plans*

Independent Practice (20 min)	
Explore policing in the United States, its history and culture, and the current reform demands **Jigsaw Reading Activity**: Create groups; each group will receive a different article to read and analyze. Each member of the group has a role while they read: 1. Illustrator: finds a way to visually represent the main themes of the text. 2. Note-taker: writes down key points and group opinions on the author's use of evidence, reasoning and possible biases. 3. Investigator: underlines and looks up new vocabulary that the team doesn't know. 4. Analyst: reads the reading out loud to the group, and shares out to the class when we come back together the group's main findings from the text using evidence. • Students can self-select roles; confirm with students their responsibilities. • Groups should read independently; circulate to ensure students are on task and fulfilling their roles' responsibilities. • Opportunities for extension will be to push groups finished early to refine their points, find a key quote that summarizes the article, and double check if their evidence matches their argument.	**Jigsaw reading activity** • Group 1: *History/origins of Police* (*TIME*) • Group 2: *Defund the Police* (*The Atlantic*) • Group 3: *The Culture of Policing* (*The Atlantic*) – provide students the abridged text • Student notebooks • PowerPoint slides
Guided Practice (40 min)	
• Following students' reading, the analyst of each group will share out the main points of the reading to the class and cite textual evidence to support the author's main argument. As each analyst is sharing, every student must write down one question for each of the other groups about what they read and what it means (2 questions total per student). • Following the share-out of each group, we will arrange our seats into Socratic seminar formation. Students will have a Socratic seminar based on the questions students wrote down. Students will use a talking stick. A volunteer begins by asking their first question and students raise their hands to receive the talking stick to participate.	• Three articles • Socratic Seminar self-grading rubric

Closing (10 min)	

• Students will summarize what they learned in the first lesson by filling out our graphic organizer. Each box in the organizer has to include a reference to one of the texts, which is how students demonstrate mastery of the objective.
• We will close out by doing a think/pair/share
 	
  • Students write down their own ideas first into the graphic organizer (3 min)
  • Students share with their elbow partner what they wrote (2 min)
  • Students share out what they wrote and where they agreed/disagreed (5 min)
 	
• As students share, they will be asked to state the significance of their findings. What does it mean for policing culture that guns are legal in our country? How does the evolution of the police through the last two centuries affect the way they operate today? How is policing linked to the institution of slavery? How do each of your findings relate to what is going on today across the country?
	• Graphic Organizer

Additional Materials

Cultures of Policing Graphic Organizer

	Historical Evolution: How has the institution of the police and its purpose evolved throughout history?	*Social Context: What are some important features of the country that may affect policing? (E.g. gun laws, demographics, history)*	*Police Institutions: How does the institution of the police currently work in the country? (E.g. training, role in society, jobs, etc.)*	*Current State of Affairs: How do citizens of this country feel about the police? Are there movements pushing for reform?*
United States				
Canada				
Norway				
Brazil				

Appendix Four
Global Collaborative Connections

Adapted from *Teachers Guide to Online Collaboration*

Global Connections for Teachers and Students

Creating collaborative experiences for students can have powerful effects on several aspects of their learning. When they make connections with their peers, whether they are on the other side of the world or only a few hundred miles away makes a difference. By establishing a human connection many educators have noted that both motivation and curiosity to learn about other cultures goes up, particularly as they learn to work on collaborative projects. Following are just some of the leading platforms that simply and easily facilitate student exchanges.

Belouga

Belouga was founded in 2017 with the mission of making education impactful and accessible on a global scale through peer-to-peer and classroom connection, communication and collaboration. Powered by

> CLAI (Curiosity, Learning, Action, Impact), Belouga provides students and teachers with a wealth of real-world learning initiatives, sourced from global organizations and customized to their educational goals and curiosity, followed by action items where they can put their learning to work in their own communities to create impact.

> https://belouga.org/

Centre for Global Education (CGE)

The Centre for Global Education develops and delivers virtual, collaborative learning projects that engage and empower youth as global citizens, through connecting them to the people, places and issues they are learning by providing global learning opportunities, enhanced through technology, informed by sound research and innovative teaching. Through a series of strategic relationships, the Centre has uniquely placed itself as an international hub of technology innovation, higher learning and global education. *(Grades 7–12)*

> http://tcge.tiged.org/

ePals

ePals enriches K-12 learning in the classroom to create real-world, culturally enriching learning experiences for students. With ePals classroom matching, teachers can connect their classes with other classes around the world who are interested in collaborating on a special project together. More and more teachers who use ePals are choosing to connect their classes through Skype, as well as a variety of other social media platforms. *(Grades K-12)*

Empatico

Empatico is a free tool for educators developed by the KIND foundation to connect their classrooms with others around the world. As Lori Gracey writes, "Teachers will save time as they no longer have to toggle between applications to connect with other interested teachers, schedule a connection, and find the right activities." The group is focused on ages 6–11 combining live video with activities designed to foster meaningful connections among students ages 6–11. *(Grades 1–6)*

GoBubble

GoBubble is a safe community for kids to connect with classmates and friends. Their moderated environment saves parents and teachers time, and gives them peace of mind as every user is verified. *(Grades K-12)*

iEARN

iEARN was founded in 1988 at the height of the cold war and as an effort to ease tensions between the Soviet Union and the US through student exchanges. Since then iEARN has pioneered online school linkages and now forms a network of 30,000 schools and youth organizations in more than 140 countries. Now headquartered in Spain it hosts over two million students a day who engage in collaborative project work worldwide. *(Grades K-12)*

TakingITGlobal

At TakingITGlobal for Educators (*TIGed*), classrooms are empowered to understand and act collaboratively on the world's greatest challenges. They do this by supporting educators to utilize technology to create transformative learning experiences for their students. Through this work, classrooms everywhere become actively engaged and connected in shaping a more inclusive, peaceful and sustainable world. *(Grades K-12)*

Global Nomads

Global Nomads Group (*GNG*) fosters dialogue and understanding among the world's youth. Founded in 1988, connecting classrooms using video conferencing technology, it has conducted programs in 60 countries reaching one million students across seven continents. Targeted at middle and high school students in the US and the Middle East, its signature "Campfire" program uses a curriculum that promotes collaboration that helps break down stereotypes and address common community issues.

Other Resources

Student Diplomacy Corps

The Student Diplomacy Corps (SDC) creates opportunities for underserved high school students from across the nation to access dynamic international education summer programs that build college readiness, deepen empathy and unleash the potential of youth.

https://sdcorps.org/welcome/

132 *Global Collaborative Connections*

Intercultural Learning Hub (HubICL)

The HubICL is designed to meet the specific needs of each audience of students and teachers. For example, a user may do any or all of the following: contribute research to the repository, answer a question in the forum, create a group of scholars with which to work on a project, and/or find ICL tools to use in the classroom.

I-Earn Global Learning Circles

I-EARN Global Learning Circles are highly interactive, project-based partnerships among a small number of schools located throughout the world. There are two sessions each year, September–January and January–May.

Global Education Motivators (GEM)

Global Education Motivators was founded in 1981 as a 501(c)(3) educational non-profit organization by former high school world cultures teacher Wayne Jacoby. GEM's original goals were to foster a deeper understanding of our evermore interdependent and interconnected world and "bring the real world into the classroom" through teacher training workshops and student-focused programs. In 1986 GEM became a NGO (a non-governmental organization) in close association with the UN Department of Public Information (now Department of Global Communications). Founder and executive director Wayne Jacoby received the UN Peace Messenger Award.

Global Education Collaborative

The Global Education Collaborative was started in 2007 by Lucy Gray. In 2010, Steve Hargadon and Lucy renamed this community the Global Education Conference Network upon the launch of their annual online conference. Their work has expanded to include additional virtual and face-to-face events under the umbrella of GlobalEd Events (www.globaledevents.com/).

Global Cities

Global Cities, Inc., a Program of Bloomberg Philanthropies, is a non-profit dedicated to connecting cities around the world and developing global competence among the next generation through its Global Scholars digital exchange program, which in 2019–2020 connected 17,000 students in 53 cities.

www.globalcities.org/

Global Citizens Initiative

Working directly with students, educators and schools, GCI provides educational tools and continuous community support to equip global citizens with the mindset, skills and resources necessary to be effective and ethical global leaders.

www.globalci.org

Global Scholars

Global Scholars is an initiative that forms part of the Bloomberg Global Cities Initiative and is designed to provide opportunities for 10- to 13-year-old public school students to build the global and general learning competencies explicated in the framework. The posts and projects of international peers serve as primary texts through which students learn about other cities, the common global topic they are studying, and the skills needed to solve a global problem. In 2017–2018, the program partnered with 576 teachers in 64 cities in 29 countries, enrolling 13,756 students in 602 classes – 90% of which were in public schools. The program charges no fees to participating schools.

www.globalcities.org/

SIMA Classroom

SIMA Lesson Plans inspire global learning and civic skill-building in dynamic and interactive ways. In conjunction with SIMA Films, educators can utilize them as examples, stand-alone workshops or incorporate them into pre-existing curricula across multiple disciplines and class formats. Designed in collaboration with leaders in the non-profit, civic engagement and education fields, all our lesson plans align with Common Core and International Baccalaureate Standards.

https://simaclassroom.com/sima-lesson-plans/

Bibliography

Asia Society. (2010). *International perspectives on U.S. education policy and practice: What can we learn from high-performing nations?* Retrieved from http://asiasociety.org/files/pdf/learningwiththeworld.pdf

Asia Society. (n.d.). *What is global competence?* Retrieved from https://asiasociety.org/education/what-global-competence

Bignold, W., & Gayton, W. (Eds.). (2009). *Global issues and comparative education* (Perspectives in Education Studies Series). Los Angeles, CA: Learning Matters.

Boix Mansilla, V., & Jackson, A. (2011). *Educating for global competence: Preparing our youth to engage the world.* New York: Asia Society.

Bourn, D. (Ed.). (2018). *Debates on global skills: Understanding global skills for 21st century professions* (pp. 87–109). London: Palgrave McMillan.

Brown, S. C., & Kysilka, M. L. (2008). *What every teacher should know about multicultural and global education.* Boston, MA: Pearson.

Gaudelli, W. (2016). *Global citizenship education: Everyday transcendence.* New York: Routledge.

GENE. (2018). Global education in Europe: Concepts, definitions and aims. *GENE.* Retrieved from http://gene.eu/wp-content/uploads/GENE-policy-briefing-Concepts-Definitions-for-web.pdf

Ghosh, A. (2016). *The great derangement: Climate change and the unthinkable.* Berkeley: University of Chicago Press.

Goren, H., & Yemini, M. (2017). Global citizenship education redefined: A systematic review of empirical studies on global citizenship education. *International Journal of Educational Research, 82,* 170–183.

Hanvey, R. (2004). An attainable global perspective. *The American Forum for Global Education.* Retrieved from www.globaled.org/an_att_glob_persp_04_11_29.pdf

Hicks, D. (2009). *A rationale for global education.* Retrieved from www.unesco.org/education/tlsf/mods/theme_c/popups/mod18t05s02.html

Kirkwood, T. F. (2001). Preparing teachers to teach from a global perspective. *The Delta Kappa Gamma Bulletin, 67*(2), 5–12.

Klein, J. (2017). *The global education guidebook: Humanizing K-12 classrooms worldwide through equitable partnerships.* Bloomington: Solution Tree.

Kniep, W. M. (1986). Defining a global education by its content. *Social Education, 50*(10), 437–446.

Lehtomäki, E., Moate, J., & Posti-Ahokas, H. (2019). Exploring global responsibility in higher education students' cross-cultural dialogues. *European Educational Research Journal, 18*(1).

Mansilla, V., & Jackson, E. D. A. (2011). *Educating for global competence.* Asia Society. Retrieved from http://asiasociety.org/files/book-globalcompetence.pdf

Merryfield, M. (1991). Preparing American secondary social studies teachers to teach from a global perspective. *Journal of Teacher Education, 42,* 11–20.

OECD and Asia Society. (2018). *Teaching for global competence in a rapidly changing world.* Paris: OECD. Retrieved from https://asiasociety.org/sites/default/files/inline-files/teaching-for-global-competence-in-a-rapidly-changing-world-edu.pdf

OECD. (2010). *Strong performers and successful reformers in education: Lessons from PISA for the United States* (p. 250). Retrieved from www.oecd.org/document/13/0,3343,en_2649_35845621_46538637_1_1_1_1,00.htm

Bibliography 135

OECD. (2019). *The road to integration: Education and migration, OECD reviews of migrant education.* Paris: OECD Publishing. https://doi.org/10.1787/d8ceec5d-en

Oxfam. (2015a). *Education for global citizenship: A guide for schools.* United Kingdom: Oxfam.

Oxfam. (2015b). *Global citizenship in the classroom: A guide for teachers.* United Kingdom: Oxfam.

Reimers, F. (2013). Education for improvement: Citizenship in the global public sphere. *Harvard International Review, 1*(35), 56–61.

Reimers, F. (2017). *Empowering students to improve the world in sixty lessons.* Charleston, SC: CreateSpace.

Schleicher, A. (2018). *World class: How to build a 21st-century school system, strong performers and successful reformers in education.* Paris: OECD Publishing. https://doi.org/10.1787/9789264300002-en

Suarez-Orozoco, M. (Ed.). (2007). *Learning in the global era: International perspectives on globalization and education.* Berkeley: University of California Press.

Süssmuth, R. (2008). On the need for teaching intercultural skills. In Suárez-Orozco (Ed.), *Learning in a global era: International perspectives on globalization and education.* Berkeley: University of California Press.

UNESCO. (2017). *Education for people and planet* (Global Education Monitoring Report). Paris: UNESCO.

UNESCO. (2018). *Preparing teachers for global citizenship education: A template.* Retrieved from http://unesdoc.unesco.org/images/0026/002654/265452e.pdf

Wilkerson, I. (2020). *Caste: The origins of our discontents.* New York: Random House.

Zhao, Y. (2017). *Imagining the future of global education: Dreams and nightmares.* New York: Routledge.

Zizek, S. (2009). *The parallax view.* Cambridge, MA: MIT Press.

Index

Adichie, Chimamanda Ngozi 1, 73–74, 80
Adidas 64
Adorno, Theodore 40–41
Africa 7, 24, 30, 39, 42, 45, 69, 70, 72, 74
AltSchool, San Francisco 11
American Civil Liberties Union (ACLU) 84
Amnesty International 35
Appadurai, Arjun 9
Apple 9, 11, 33, 57, 58
Arendt, Hannah 85
Ashoka (Emperor) 8
Asian (workers) 66
Asia Society 18, 93, 94, 95, 97, 99, 100, 102
Association of International Educators 36; *see also* NAFSA
Auschwitz 40
Australia 2, 35, 100

Bali (Green School) 10
Barrett, Martyn 28, 88, 91n13
Barth, Roland 92
BBC 64, 85, 86
Belgium 45; *see also* King Leopold
Billion, Didier 11
Binder, Sean 55
Black Death 103
Black Lives Matter 24, 46, 65, 127
Black Spartacus 77; *see also* Louverture, Toussaint
Bosnia 41
Boix Mansilla, Veronica 31, 88
British 64, 65, 74, 77
Buddhism 82

Calvino, Italo 77
Canada 95, 96, 99, 111, 125, 126, 129
Carson, Rachel 15, 16, 17; *see also* Silent Spring
caste 38, 40, 44
certificates, global 97
Cheney, Lynn 21
child labor 32, 33, 51, 57
Chile 45
China 7, 8, 38, 43, 44, 66, 71n7, 101n8
Cicero 52
Cinco de Mayo 99
citizenship, global 50, 58, 95

Civil War, American 32
Clark, Josh 3
Clarkson, Thomas 42
Clavell, James 65; *see also* Shogun
colonialism 38, 44
Columbus 39
Confucius 3, 8
co-operative learning 28
Cortes, Hernado 39
cosmopolitanism 50–51
COVID-19 20, 82, 102
Cuba 3
cultural diversity 7, 11

Darwin, Charles 104
DDT 15
Denmark Ørestad Gymnasium 11, 25
Depression, The Great 102
Dewey, John 16, 17
Diogenes 3, 52
Disney 75
DNA 3
Donne, John 3
DRC (Democratic Republic of the Congo) 58
Drew, Chris 95

Eltham High School, Melbourne, Australia 100
Emerson, Ralph Waldo 103
Empatico 89, 131
Environmental Protection Agency (EPA) 16
ePals 89
Equiano, or Gustav Vassa 42
Ethiopia 86
European (migrant crisis) 56

Facebook 65, 76, 84, 86
Finland High school (South Tapiola) 10, 25
Floyd, George 46
Franklin Delano Roosevelt (FDR) 53
Freinet, Celestin 87
French Revolution 7
Fukushima (Japan) 64

Gates Foundation 39
Germany 8, 34, 37n8, 41, 45, 88

Index 137

Ghosh, Amitav 34
Global (North & South) 1, 13, 20, 34, 38, 39, 45, 46, 48
global certificate 97–98
Global Studies Diploma 98
global supply chain 58
Grand Tour 18
Great Britain 47, 68
greenwashing 70–71

Hannah-Jones, Nikole (*1619 project*) 74
Hanvey, Robert 17, 24, 25, 28, 29, 67
Harari, Yuval 1, 7, 23, 57
Harris, Kamala, Vice President 28
Heick, Terry 93
Hickel, Jason 44–46
Hidden Figures (movie) 78
Hierocles 51–52, 75
History of the World in 100 Objects 76; *see also* McGregor, Neil
Holocaust 53, 68
Honduras 48

I-EARN 132
IKEA 63
India 7, 9, 28, 44, 114
International Baccalaureate (IB) 133
International Women's Day 99
Internet 36, 47, 50, 57, 82, 83, 84, 87, 88, 93, 101
Iran 45, 115
Islam 21

Jackson, Anthony, President of the Asia Society 17, 88
Jacobs, A.J. 76
Japan 64–65, 99, 114
Jesus 3, 8
Jews 55, 68, 80, 103

Kaetsu Ariake Junior & Senior High School, Japan 99
Kahneman, Daniel 77; *see also Thinking, Fast and Slow*
Kant, Immanuel 52–53, 55
Karate 63
Kentucky Fried Chicken (KFC) 64
kick boxing 63
King, Martin Luther 1, 59
King Leopold 45; *see also* Belgium
KitKat (Japanese obsession) 64
Klein, Naomi 63, 76
Knight, Phil 63

labor, child 111
Landrieu, Mitch 47
Las Casas 3
Lesbos 109
Louverture, Toussaint 77

Mandela, Nelson 46
McCourt, Frank 43

McDonalds 68
McGregor, Neil 76; *see also History of the world in 100 Objects*
Merkel, Angela, German Chancellor 34–35
middle passage 43
mission statement 94–95
Montezuma 39
Moore, Sir Thomas (play) 78–80; *see also* Shakespeare, William
Morrison, Toni 31
Mossadegh, PM Iran 45
Mulgrave School, Vancouver, British Columbia 99
multicultural 11
Muslim(s) 69, 75; *see also* Islam
Myanmar 55

NAFSA 36; *see also* Association of International Educators
National Trust 47
Native Americans 74, 39, 80n5
Nazi Germany 41
Needham High School in Needham, MA 98
Nestle 64
news 60
New York Times (*1619 Project*) 74
Nigeria 74
Nike 33, 63–64, 65, 66–67
Nuremberg Laws 44
Nussbaum, Martha 70

Obama, Barack, President 28
OECD (Organization for Economic Development) 27, 30, 35, 96
Olathe Kansas School District 98
Opium Wars 44
Orwell, George 46
Othello 31; *see also* Shakespeare, William
othering 40–41, 49n5, 75, 78, 82
Oxfam 59

Papua, New Guinea 35
PISA (Programme for International Student Assessment) 19, 25, 26, 29, 93, 96–97
Plutarch 52
Pocahontas and John Smith 39
Power, Samantha 80
project work, project based learning 33
Project Zero 31, 32
Providence Day School, Charlotte NC 98

Qatar 73, 80

Rakhine State 41
Ramadan 75
refugee crisis 55
Reimers, Fernando 18, 20, 58, 97
Rohingya 41, 90n8
role play simulations 57
Roman Empire 7
Roosevelt, Eleanor 53

138 *Index*

Roosevelt, Franklin 53; *see also* Franklin Delano Roosevelt (FDR)
Rovelli, Carlo 103
Rwanda 41

Seneca 52
Shakespeare, William 31, 78–80
Shogun 65; *see also* Clavell, James
Silent Spring 15; *see also* Carson, Rachel
simulations 47
slave narrative 41–42, 103
slave/slavery 33, 38, 39–49, 51, 56–57, 66, 72–74, 77, 80, 102, 103, 129
smartphones 82
social media 57
South Africa 69–70
Sri Lanka 86
Starbucks 57, 63, 65
Steve Jobs high school 11
student newspaper (international) 94
supply chain (global) 58
Sushi 64–65
Syria 55, 103

Teachout, Zephyr 86
Tett, Gillian 64
Thinking, Fast and Slow (book by Daniel Kahneman) 77
Thunberg, Greta 2, 4n7

Tichnor-Wagner, Ariel 90
TikTok 68
Timmerman, Kelsey 9
Toffler, Alvin 8, 13
travel projects 34
Truman, Harry (Four Points Speech) 45
Trump, Donald (Fake News) 84
Turkey 48

United Nations 2, 45, 98
United States 32, 36, 43, 45, 66, 74, 110, 111, 115, 125, 127, 128, 129
Universal Declaration of Human Rights 50, 53, 55, 57

Walmart 66, 71
War, World 7, 16, 43, 45
Wilkerson, Isabel 1, 44
Wohlleben, Peter 104
World Bank 10, 39, 46, 121
World Cup 73
World Trade Center 51
World Water Day 99
Wright, Isabel 74

Xboxes 63

Zizek, Slavoj 12
Zuckerberg, Mark 86

9780367643140